Archive Publicat

CW01668500

Grimsby Evening Telegraph

GY 80
RAPALLO
REMINDO

Grand Old Ladies

Steve Richards

First Published 1990
Archive Publications Ltd
10 Seymour Court
Manor Park
RUNCORN
Cheshire

in association with

Grimsby Evening Telegraph, 80 Cleethorpe Road,
GRIMSBY
South Humberside

©1990 Text Steve Richards
©1990 Photographs Grimsby Evening Telegraph
©1990 Arrangement Archive Publications Ltd

ISBN 0 948946 68 7

All text is taken from newspaper articles from the 'Grand Old Ladies' series, which appeared in the *Grimsby Evening Telegraph* during the early 80s.

©1990 Lyrics, Maypole Music, for all countries, London NW11 OSA and ©1968 March Music/Hedley Music Group.
All rights reserved.

1. ***previous page:*** *Comings and Goings. The Fish Docks were never quiet. Even during the afternoon when the tide was low there was always plenty to do. This photograph, which dates from 1954 or 1955 shows trawlers being moved in readiness for sailing or brief spells of maintenance.*
2. ***below:*** *It was a hard life even ashore. These lumpers were pictured at work on the pontoon some 40 years ago. These were the days before mechanised unloading and the fish, stored in the tough wicker baskets, were dragged ashore across ice-covered boards.*

CONTENTS

3. On the way home, 1932. This photograph shows the crew of the Berenga, an 87-ton coal burner built during the First World War which was brought to Grimsby in 1925 by Crampins for work in the North Sea. The photograph was supplied by Len Horsefield, pictured second from the right on the front row. He was then third hand on the Berenga and was to spend 20 years at sea as a fisherman.

Introduction

You could just make her out in the early morning mist . . . the heavily-laden trawler standing off Cleethorpes in the mouth of the Humber. She was low in the water as she waited for the tide to complete the last leg of a journey which had begun three weeks earlier and during which the rust-streaked vessel and its 16-man crew had been through ordeals that would make most of us blanch.

That trawler had braved mountainous waves, hurricane-force winds and the worst enemy of all — ice — on its trip to the edge of the Arctic Circle, and all to feed the voracious appetite of a nation raised on fish and chips.

Her fish rooms were crammed with 2,000 kits of the finest haddock and shelf cod, 125 tons of prime fish packed in ice and soon to be on its way to the fish and chip shops for Bradford, Barnsley and Birmingham.

On board most of the crew were standing on the fo'c'sle, anxious to catch their first sight of England for 21 days, their thoughts on home, pay packets and the Freeman Street pubs, though not necessarily in that order. The skipper was on the bridge, filling in the last report for the owners on another trip.

An hour later the engine room telegraph would ring and the chief engineer would respond. The last leg began. The lock gates would swing open and the trawler would nudge her way in, watched by a huddled group of wives and children. She would head for a berth alongside one of the quays where, that night, the lumpers would swarm on board and begin man-handling the catch ashore.

The balance sheet would later show the profits and losses for the trip. The price of the catch would be weighed against the costs of the voyage: the coal

4. Working the northern trawl. Backs bowed, faces grim, the crew of a Grimsby trawler begin to sort the catch after a haul off Iceland in the 1950s.

burnt, the food eaten, the wages and poundage paid to the crew. If the ink on the bottom of the page was black then everyone was happy. If it was red then there would be anxious faces on Fish Dock Road and hungry children in half a dozen back-to-back homes over the next few weeks.

But whatever happened, that trawler and those 16 men would soon be back at sea again, in the case of the men within a couple of days if their money had run out.

This was the only life thousands of men knew in Grimsby right up till the politics of the Seventies finally killed an industry.

But now all that is nothing more than a memory. The trawlers have long gone, most to the scrapyard, the more cost-effective ones to oil rig supply work. Men still talk in the pubs and clubs of Grimsby and Cleethorpes with affection of the "good old days", of standing watch in a force 10 on the Black Watch off Iceland, or fishing round the clock off the North Cape in the summer on the Grimsby Town.

Dominating all those memories are the trawlers themselves. Almost always dirty, rusty, weather-battered vessels reeking of the trade they were in, they acquired the same kind of romantic affection as those steam locomotives to whose generation they belonged. Like the steam engines, each had a character of its own. Deep sea fishermen will tell you that even if two vessels were built side-by-side in the same yard from virtually the same set of drawings, each trawler would have its own characteristics.

To those same fishermen the trawlers became almost living, breathing entities. Some were loved, others were loathed. Some were superb sea-going vessels, others tossed and rolled like stricken cows.

They were individuals and the legends grew about them.

Every trawler had its own story to tell, a story of drama on the high seas, of good fortune, a story of tragedy or bad luck. These are just some of those stories.

5. Another bumper catch. The nets are bulging with fish, the decks already piled high with the day's catch. It looked like another good day's work for those Grimsby fishermen pictured here on an unamed trawler.

Saved !

The Wolverhampton Wanderers

It was on 22 December 1957 that the Grimsby trawler *Wolverhampton Wanderers* fought her way through a violent storm and heavy seas into the history book. The 536-ton trawler saved the 14-man crew of the merchant ship *Bosworth* in what remains one of the most dramatic sea rescues ever mounted by a Grimsby vessel. And it brought honour for both the trawler's skipper, Bob Drew, and her crew.

The *Wolverhampton Wanderers* was built in Beverley in 1946 for Boston Deep Sea Fisheries of Hull and was originally named the *St Matthew*. She was one of the first vessels to be built specifically for oil burning. The 166ft trawler was to fish out of Canada for a few years but was eventually bought by Consolidated Fisheries in December 1956. She made one trip, to Iceland for Consols under her old name and skippered by Bill Smith, before becoming the *Wolverhampton Wanderers*. She concentrated her fishing mainly on the north-west coast of Iceland and proved to be a good sea ship, well liked by her crew. She was originally fitted with Marconi radar but this was eventually changed to a Decca system which was standard in Consols. Her career was uneventful until the events of 22 December 1957.

The merchant vessel *Bosworth*, with a 14-man crew aboard, was bound from Granton in Scotland to Sweden with a cargo of coals. As the weather conditions deteriorated she called for other shipping to stand by as she had developed a heavy list. A number of vessels in the area including the *Wolverhampton Wanderers* and a Glasgow ship, the *Narva*, quickly responded and headed for the scene.

Force 11

Skipper Bob Drew, recalled what happened. "We were about 120 miles on our way to the White Sea grounds when the storm forced us to round and dodge back towards Grimsby. We heard the distress message from the *Bosworth* and of course we must have been blowing about force 11 at the

6. The Wolverhampton Wanderers.

7. *The Wolverhampton Wanderers.*

time," he said. The trawler tried to make good speed but found she was shipping too much water. "It eventually took us five hours to do just 30 miles. When we got to the *Bosworth* she had a 20 degree list to starboard and was taking water all over her starboard side.

"We kept a searchlight trained on her all night. In the early hours we got a message from her crew saying that she was sinking and could we take the crew off," said Skipper Drew. The *Wolverhampton Wanderers* was manoeuvred alongside and went broadside to the wind. She too began taking water as she was mercilessly lashed by the heavy seas and storm force winds.

"We got liferafts ready with lines on. But we could not get the lines aboard the *Bosworth* to make the transfer," said Skipper Drew. Then with the two vessels very close together the seas took a hand in the matter. The waves lifted the *Bosworth* high in the water and crashed her down on top of the *Wolverhampton Wanderer*'s starboard bulwarks, causing extensive damage. A further wave caused the two vessels to part. "I shouted to them at this stage to take to their boats.

Oil Aid

"We picked them up in about 20 minutes. I managed to go right alongside and pick them up. A liner in the area spread oil on the water to help. It was only diesel oil but it did have some effect. We also managed to pick up the *Bosworth*'s boats as well," said Skipper Drew. Later the Hull trawler *Faraday* arrived on the scene and eventually managed to get the *Bosworth* into tow, having achieved the difficult task of putting four men aboard her. She was towed into Aberdeen with the *Wolverhampton Wanderers* acting as escort vessel.

"The *Bosworth*'s crew would not go back aboard her. I wanted to put them back on board but they did not like the idea," said Skipper Drew. It took 10 days for the *Wolverhampton Wanderers* to be repaired. But the rescue had its tragic side as well. The *Narva* (1,991 tons) with a 28-man crew sank while on her way to the *Bosworth*. Despite a frantic search by aircraft and ships all the crew was lost. For Skipper Drew it was not his first rescue. At the end of 1956 when he was in command of the trawler *Derby County* he towed another Grimsby vessel, the *Neath Castle*, to safety after she ran aground in the Faroes. The *Stoke City* also helped in the tow. On 24 February Skipper Drew and the crew of the *Wolverhampton Wanderers* were the guests at a presentation to honour their gallant *Bosworth* rescue. Skipper Drew and his officers received waterproof wristwatches from the collier's owners while the rest of the crew got cigarette lighters.

The Crew

The full crew was Skipper Drew; mate Mr B Donnelly; chief engineer Mr J Ritchie; second engineer Mr L Nuttall; third hand Mr P Reader; deckhands R Valentine, G French, G Butterill, M Peters, J Forrest, B Scott, M Walsh, H Cook; firemen E Delatouche and J Harwood; trimmers J Taylor, W Tyas; cook L Finch; wireless operator D Parker; galley boy D Burgess.

Skipper Drew and mate Mr Donnelly were also awarded the Emile Robin Award for 1957 by the Shipwrecked Fishermen and Mariners Benevolent Society. The rescue also led to a legal battle when the owners of the *Wolverhampton Wanderers* and the *Faraday* took action against the *Bosworth*'s owners for salvage services. Eventually the Grimsby vessel was awarded £11,400 and the *Faraday* £8,260. Skipper Drew has fond memories of his old charge. "She was a good sea ship and a good fishing ship," he said.

Mr Harry Hutson, of Little Michael Street, Grimsby, spent a period as radio officer aboard the trawler. "She made good steady earnings, but Consol's ships were not renowned for breaking records. She concentrated on quality Iceland plaice, haddock and cod. She was a good sea ship, well liked by the crew," said Mr Hutson. He remembered the trawler being involved in the first Cod War with Iceland in September 1958. "We were very close to the end of our trip and spent the last few days in a box area protected by the Navy frigate HMS *Palliser* and accompanied by two Icelandic gunboats," said Mr Hutson.

Boarding

And he remembers one particular incident involving one of the Northern fleet of trawlers operating from Grimsby. The vessel — the name of which Mr Hutson couldn't recall — was boarded by an Icelandic gunboat. HMS *Palliser* put her own boarding party on board and removed the Icelanders.

"I was listening to it all over the radio telephone aboard the *Wolves*. The Icelandic vessel refused to take its own boarding party from *Palliser*. *Palliser* had no choice and put them into their sea boat at a discreet distance from the shore and let them row home," said Mr Hutson. HMS *Palliser* had been on the other side of the protective box when the incident occurred.

The *Wolverhampton Wanderers*, on the other hand, could see the incident taking place and helped identify the Northern boat though there was thick fog in the area. "The *Palliser* came on the air saying: "Keep a good look out for us, we are steaming at 12 knots." A few minutes later it was 15 knots, then 18 knots and so on until she was doing well over 20 knots in the fog — quite hair-raising," described Mr Hutson. The radio operator of the Northern boat barricaded himself in the wireless room and the chief engineer went so far as to start dismantling the engines! The *Wolverhampton Wanderers* was the first Grimsby ship to land at home after the outbreak of the conflict. Mr Hutson's last trip aboard her was under Skipper Drew to the White Sea grounds. The weather was very good for most of the trip and they caught 850 kits of plaice quite quickly. It was landed in Grimsby in early October 1958 and grossed over £8,000.

8. The crew of the Wolverhampton Wanderers when they received their awards for rescuing the crew of the Bosworth, shortly before Christmas 1957. Skipper Bob Drew is centre front.

Worry

Mr Reg Swann, of Tunnard Street, Grimsby, had a spell as chief engineer aboard the vessel — from February 1957 until June 1960. He had memories of yet another heartstopping episode aboard her.

It was New Year's Day 1960 when the trawler was steaming north and was off the Norway coast. A force eight gale was blowing and suddenly there was a problem with the oil supply to the engine. A piece of metal had become so hot it had melted. Mr Swann and second engineer Jack Taylor went to work with a block and tackle to replace the broken part. But things were not made any easier by the storm conditions or the fact that the *Wolverhampton Wanderers* was drifting closer and closer to shore.

"It took us about three and a half hours. By this time we were only about three miles off the coast and everyone was starting to get a little worried," recalled Mr Swann. Of the trawler he said: "She was a good ship and she was a lucky ship."

The *Wolverhampton Wanderers* continued her career until the late 1960s when she became one of the first post war-built vessels to be scrapped.

The Leicester City

The *Leicester City* tragedy 31 years ago changed the whole way of life of a young galley boy — persuading him to leave the sea and become one of Grimsby's best known butchers. And the toss of a coin could possibly have saved the life of his brother, Harold.

Mr Archie Needham, who now runs a chain of butchers' shops throughout the area, was just 16 at the time of the tragic grounding of the *Leicester City*, off the Island of Hoy in March 1953. He had done one previous trip on the trawler *Visenda*. "I spun a coin with my brother Harold to see which one of us would go on the *Leicester City*. Fortunately I was a better swimmer than he was," he explained. The trawler ran aground in the early hours of the morning. In the pitch black the crew did not realise they were close to shore and as the vessel listed the skipper gave the order to abandon ship.

Saw Lamp

"I remember going down a rope which burned my hands. We were in the sea quite a long time. We finally managed to get ashore about 5 am in the morning," said Mr Needham. He explained how swimming training in Grimsby Docks had stood him in good stead. "But it was pretty cold. I remember that later we had to go down to the Mission to identify the bodies."

"As soon as I got back to Grimsby my mother got me a butcher's bike in Freeman Street and I never went fishing again."

"I always remember the incident because it was the Derby the day before. I believe a horse called *Early Mist* had won," recalled Mr Needham.

The disaster claimed the lives of seven fishermen. Eleven men survived. At 7.10 pm on 25 March the survivors came home — in borrowed clothes, some with their feet bandaged and covered in thick socks. Their feet had been badly cut by the jagged rocks. The train journey back from Scotland had taken 36 hours. Relatives had maintained a 24-hour vigil at the station. The men were met by the outside manager for Consolidated Fisheries — the vessel's owners — Mr Jack Mawers. Six days after the grounding it was still uncertain whether the *Leicester City* could be salvaged.

Salvage

But just a few days later came the first hint that the trawler might be a total write-off. She was battered by the bad weather and eventually a salvage vessel which had been standing by, the *Salveda*, was withdrawn. The trawler was eventually abandoned. There was happier news on 20 May 1953 when the *Evening Telegraph* reported that the lifeboatmen who had gone to help the

SALMON TROUT

Wipe and draw the trout, but do not scale it, put on a drainer in a fish kettle, sprinkle with lemon juice and salt, cover with water containing salt, and simmer for about 20 minutes. Serve with Dutch sauce

vessel were to receive awards from the Royal National Lifeboat Institution. The Stromness vessel had picked up 14 of the crew, although three died. Coxswain William Sinclair, of Stromness, and Coxswain Angus MacIntosh, of Thurso, both received the Institution's thanks inscribed on vellum. The awards were given for "the determination, skill and initiative" shown by them in finding all the missing men in treacherous tidal water and for most of the time in dense fog.

Moving

On 22 October 1953 there was another moving presentation in Grimsby. The mate of the *Leicester City*, John Youngs, had died after bravely swimming ashore from the stranded vessel to get help. On 17 November 1952 he had qualified for his skipper's certificate. But when it came to the prizegiving it was his nine-year-old son Edward who walked onto the stage of the Grimsby Nautical School. He was presented with the barometer which should have been handed to his father as the oldest man on the skippers' course. At a subsequent public inquiry into the loss of the *Leicester City* Sheriff D B Keith said it was quite clear the accident was not attributable to lack of care or to negligence.

Skipper Osmund Johansen was cleared of any blame. He had taken the vessel because her regular skipper Bill Hardie was unavailable. His wife, Mrs Dolly Hardie, explained that as a Lt Commander of the Royal Naval Reserve her husband had been required to go to Portsmouth to take part in Naval drills. "I can remember it well. A steward came through to the dining room and told Bill there was a call for him. When he came back he told me the *Leicester City* had gone aground and some men were missing," said Mrs Hardie.

The vessel's wireless operator, Mr Michael Dimopoulous, who was one of the men lost, was remembered by one of his radio colleagues, Mr Harry

9. Some of the Leicester City survivors with the crew of the Stromness lifeboat.

Hutson, of Little Michael Street, Grimsby. At the time of the disaster, Mr Hutson was sailing aboard the Grimsby trawler *Hekla*. He and Mr Dimopoulous did their usual radio check the night before.

Message

"After the schedule was over Mick passed me a coded message to be delivered by hand to his home in Cleethorpes. Later that morning I heard the sad news that the *Leicester City* had run ashore and Mick was missing presumed drowned and later that his body had been recovered by the lifeboat.

"We docked on Sunday evening and I was undecided whether or not to deliver the message to his home. I decided to go ahead and deliver it but no one was home so I slipped it through the letter box. My ship sailed again on Wednesday morning and ever since I have wondered if I did the right thing," said Mr Hutson.

Nasty Fire

Mr William Brown, of Sandringham Road, Cleethorpes, told how his father, Skipper Jack Brown, had commanded several of the "football" class trawlers. And he recalled how after being converted from coal to diesel shortly before her grounding, the *Leicester City* had a nasty fire on board.

"It was my father and crew that went to her aid, located her in a violent snowstorm and took her in tow," said Mr Brown. He believed his father was skipper of the *Cardiff Castle* at the time.

Mrs M Stubbs, of White Road, North Thoresby, remembered even further back than that. Her father, the late Mr Fred Panton, was chief engineer on the *Leicester City* during the late 1930s.

"Amongst the crew was Mr Frank Bray, Mr George Ayers and I believe the skipper was Mr Hutchinson. Although I was a small child I can remember my father taking me on board. And I remember the sorrow in the household when the news came on the radio that the *Leicester City* was missing.

10, 11, 12. ***below, opposite page and overleaf:*** *The Leicester City battered by bad weather.*

"After waiting for further news we heard that there had been a mistake and in fact it was the *Leicestershire*."

That trawler was also lost at the Island of Hoy on 28 January 1938.

When the Grimsby trawler *Leicester City* ran aground, busy streets thronged with shoppers were stilled as the funeral cortege, almost half-a-mile long, wound its way through the streets on the way to Scartho Cemetery. At the entrance to the cemetery nine survivors of the disaster formed a guard of honour.

The respect shown that day was due testament to the regard in which the dead fishermen and their colleagues were held. Hundreds of people had waited outside the Bethel Mission in Tiverton Street, Cleethorpes, as Port Missioner Mr Albert Broughton told those squeezed inside that the service of the seven men had not been wasted.

"We are sharing your grief," he told the families.

Hit Rocks

The vessel was on her way home from the Icelandic fishing grounds when she hit the rocks off the Island of Hoy in the Orkneys. In the darkness the crew were unaware that they were only 200 yards from the shore. Shortly after her grounding the vessel developed a heavy list to starboard and Skipper Osmund Johansen gave the order to abandon ship.Skipper Johansen had given the order to go full astern.

"But it was too late. We had just started going astern when we touched. When she started to list I told them it was every man for himself," he said. Before going over the side the crew lit flares. The skipper and nine men took to a lifeboat but it overturned. Other men were swept from their rafts by the rough seas.

Flares

Crofters on Hoy saw the flares and alerted the lifeboats at Stromness and

Thurso. Two hours later Stromness lifeboat picked up four exhausted men clinging to a raft in Hoy Sound. One of them died before the boat reached Stromness. In the meantime the *Leicester City*'s lifeboat, the skipper and the men still clinging to it, had drifted ashore. The mate, Mr Edward Youngs, the strongest swimmer of the group, heroically struck out for help when the boat first overturned. He managed to reach the shore where he was found dead from exposure and exhaustion.

At daybreak the search for survivors was joined by an RAF Hastings and went on all day. It was late on Sunday night that the last missing man, wireless operator Michael Alexander Dimopoulous (26), was found by Thursoe lifeboat. He was dead.

Lifeboat

Skipper Johansen recalled that at 5 am the crofters went to the lifeboat and found third hand Eric Howard still sitting in there.

"I remember that when they got him inside his hands were so cold that he put them in the fire. The coal stuck to his hand but he was not even burned. I will always remember that," he said.

Conditions on the night were terrible. "It was the surf that did all the damage," said Skipper Johansen. He said he had given the order to abandon ship because of the nasty list which the trawler had developed.

Dropsy

Just how close the vessel was to the shore was not discovered until much later in the day when bright sunshine dispersed the thick fog which had shrouded the vessel. Then the *Leicester City* was seen to have righted herself and was standing on an even keel.

Ironically, if the crew had stayed aboard they could have been taken off by the lifeboat in daylight without difficulty. Skipper Johansen, who had been suffering from dropsy at the time of the grounding, finished up with his feet very badly damaged. He was treated at a Post Office on Hoy which also served as a hospital.

"My feet were cut wide open and I had septic poisoning," he said. A former Hull man, Skipper Johansen, who was 34 when the disaster happened, came to Grimsby in 1949. He was based at Grimsby for a time while in command of a naval minesweeper.

The Dead

He remembered: "There was no panic. I had a magnificent crew. Some of them had followed me from my previous ship."

The Lord Ernle

The quick thinking of a radio "ham" who also happened to be the harbour master at Bridlington brought rescue for the 15-man crew of the Grimsby trawler *Lord Ernle*, stranded on notorious rocks on the Yorkshire coast.

It was a lucky escape indeed for only a few months before the Hull trawler *Skegness* had run aground at almost the identical spot with the loss of all hands. News of the *Lord Ernle*'s demise reached Grimsby on 3 March 1937. And there was news too of the spirited action of the trawler's wireless operator Mr Stephen Codling who continued to send out bright, breezy messages which served to spur the rescuers to greater efforts. And there was praise for the crew of the Flamborough lifeboat who eventually pulled off the dramatic rescue. The *Lord Ernle* was a vessel of some 325 tons, built in 1919 and owned by the Perihelion Steam Fishing Company of Grimsby.

On the night of 2 March 1937, at around 9.30 pm, she ran into thick fog off the Yorkshire coast and, blinded by the conditions, ran aground around 11.15 pm. Skipper Arthur "The Shadow" Phillipson was in command of the vessel and told reporters later that 15 minutes after the trawler hit the rocks the lights had failed. Skipper Phillipson himself climbed up the mast and set fire to some fishnetting to act as a flare. Meanwhile as the crew wondered if they were going to be rescued and heavy seas continued to pound the trawler the ship's SOS had been picked up just a few miles away in the port of Bridlington. Luckily the man on the receiving end of the message was none other than the Bridlington harbour master, Lt E Taylor, who had the amateur radio gear set up at his home in George's Avenue. As he turned the dials he caught the alarming message from the *Lord Ernle*. It said briefly: "In immediate danger. All lights out. Bumping heavily." Without hesitation he passed the message to the crew of the Bridlington lifeboat which immediately launched and went in search of the stricken vessel. The radio operator on the *Lord Ernle*, Mr Codling, kept his cool and continued to broadcast cheery messages to the rescuers. One early message he sent said: "I think the job is OK and going well but I cannot see. They have got a line on board. Cheerio." The last message he passed before leaving the battered trawler was: "I have got a call to come. I'll be seeing you sometime." The rescuers were soon on the scene rigging up lighting and trying to get a line aboard the *Lord Ernle*.

Skipper Phillipson told reporters: "The first line shot aboard by the lifeboat rocket apparatus snapped after only one of the crew had been taken off." Then the rescuers faced the problem of getting the rest of the *Lord Ernle*'s crew to safety. A dramatic account of how each of the trawler's crew jumped into the sea and was pulled aboard the lifeboat was given by wireless operator Codling. He told the *Evening Telegraph* at the time: "We were steaming slowly

13. The crew of the Lord Ernle after their rescue by Bridlington lifeboat. Seated in the centre is the lifeboat cox with Skipper Phillipson on his right.

14. The radio operator Stephen Codling, whose desperate messages spurred the rescuers to greater efforts.

in very thick weather when suddenly we struck rock. The skipper told me at once to send an SOS and I got replies from three boats on 140 metres. They were the *Boscama*, *Welbeck* and *Nordale*.

"They took our bearings. The *Boscama* was about 30 miles away and the *Nordale* was in harbour in Scarborough. She also passed our message on to the coastguards and the lifeboat. The lifeboat at Flamborough was launched and they were pretty slick in coming.

"The *Lord Ernle* was right up on the shore underneath the cliffs and the lifeboat was our only hope. There was no chance of getting ashore anywhere as we were right up on the rocks. We had a very heavy list and the ship was filling rapidly, water was bursting over the deck all the time. When the lifeboat reached the scene the crew managed to get a breeches buoy on board the *Lord Ernle*. But when the first man was being taken off one of the ropes parted and he went into the sea. They pulled him aboard the lifeboat with the other rope. They got another line fast and had four or five men aboard the lifeboat when another rope parted," said Mr Codling.

Still the rescuers persevered. They managed to get another rope connected and everyone else managed to get away from the trawler safely. "To do this we had to jump overboard with a rope tied around our waists. I could see what was going on on the trawler's deck as I was in the wireless cabin all the time. When all but five men had got away the skipper told me to stand by and I sent out a message that we were OK.

"While I was standing on the deck waiting my turn the waves were washing right over the after part of the trawler and this was the only place where the lifeboat could safely approach," said Mr Codling. Eventually the *Lord Ernle* was to be declared a total loss.

Reports told how she was breaking up under the constant pounding of the seas. Her bows remained fast at the point where they had grounded but her stern swung round towards the cliffs. That indicated that the trawler had broken her back. Her bridge, funnel and mizzen mast were all swept overboard. The *Lord Ernle*'s bottom was very badly damaged and her decks were broken. As the stormy seas surged around the vessel her plates could be heard ripping and tearing. So severe were conditions that no one was able to get aboard after the crew was taken off.

Magnetic Puzzle of Bempton Cliffs

Was the Grimsby trawler lured on to rocks off the Yorkshire coast by the wreckage of other iron-built vessels?

It was certainly one of the theories suggested to explain the loss. Some days later the iron wreckage theory was advanced in Bridlington. It was suggested that the Bempton and Speeton cliffs had perhaps become "iron-bound" owing to the large number of wrecks lying there. And it was felt that the iron could affect the compasses of other vessels, like the *Lord Ernle*, causing them to run ashore. In most cases all the wreckage had been washed away except the ship's boilers. But in one place the wreckage of a submarine lost during the war remained. The Lloyds agent in Bridlington at the time, Mr C H Gray, pointed out that several ships had gone ashore at the same place and that their masters were often puzzled as to how they got there. A Bridlington schoolmaster also agreed it was possible that the iron at the foot of the cliffs could affect ships' compasses.

Fourth Ashore

The *Lord Ernle* was the fourth vessel to go ashore at a similar spot during that particular winter. Many others had lucky escapes, touching the rocks but managing to get off. But how they hit the rocks did not concern the *Lord Ernle*'s men. They were just happy to be saved and thankful to Bridlington harbour master Lt E Taylor who had picked up their distress call on his radio.

Mate Mr Stan Whitelam (78), of Parris Place, Cleethorpes, remembers the drama well.

The *Lord Ernle* had been on her way back from the White Sea fishing grounds with some 1,200 kits of fish. The weather was filthy, with thick fog making navigation difficult. Mr Whitelam recalled that when they hit the rocks there were three or four cars on the cliffs above. "They shone their lights on us.

"We were taking water from below. The decks burst and there was fish flying around," he said. The Flamborough lifeboat was quickly on the scene but could not get close enough because of the conditions. In the end the crew of the *Lord Ernle* had to jump overboard and were pulled by line to the lifeboat.

"They pulled us aboard one by one. Once or twice the line broke. It was pretty awful," said Mr Whitelam. He told how on one occasion as the lifeboat tried to get close to the trawler it reared up sickeningly and crashed down on the Grimsby vessel. "He did some damage to the lifeboat. I think some woodwork burst," said Mr Whitelam.

After the rescue the crew were taken to a pub at Flamborough where they were given dry clothes and warmed themselves in front of a roaring fire. "The lifeboatmen enjoyed themselves. They were singing and talking about other rescues they had been involved in. A tug came and picked us up later to bring us home," said Mr Whitelam.

Mrs G Drake, of Westerdale Way, Grimsby, recalled how her father Mr Frank Moore was chief engineer aboard the *Lord Ernle*. "I remember him telling all the family how the rope snapped as the rescue was going on. My father was a big man. He weighed nearly 16 stones. But sadly to say he got

15. The Lord Ernle running aground after running into thick fog.

lost on the trawler *Wigmore*, the first Grimsby trawler lost in the war," said Mrs Drake.

After the ship grounded another Grimsby vessel, the *Welbeck*, sent a message that the whole crew was safe. During the rescue operation the men on the trawler were working in complete darkness. The *Lord Ernle* had lost one of her lifeboats on the way to the fishing grounds and had picked up a new one at Stromness. However, when they tried to launch that it began to sink as the plug holes had not been stopped up. A broom handle was placed in the hole, but was soon swept away by the seas.

Mr Arthur Corn, of Southern Walk, Scartho, was a sparehand aboard the *Lord Ernle* and at 18 her youngest crewman. When the first line to the trawler from the lifeboat was secured, Mr Corn, being the youngest, was instructed by Skipper Phillipson to go first.

"I did and unfortunately after leaving the ship the line parted and I dropped into the sea. I was in two minds as to whether to unravel myself from the breeches buoy and swim to the lifeboat or hang on to the one line left. I chose the latter, which fortunately for me proved to be the lifeboat's line.

"I was pulled through the water to the lifeboat and safety where a tot of rum was supplied. I was not much the worse for the episode," said Mr Corn. He believed the trawler's propellor must have been stripped on grounding. "If we had been in a position to reverse the engines we would have backed off into deeper water and the ship would have sunk in a very short time, taking all of us with her," he said.

The day after the incident Mr Corn, who was later to become a skipper himself, got another view of the disaster — from an aircraft. He was sufficiently recovered to fly with his cousin Geoffrey Rowbotham who was to become a squadron leader in the RAF.

"He flew men in a clapped out, dual control aircraft to view the remains of the *Lord Ernle* the day after," said Mr Corn. Some weeks later at the annual meeting of the Royal National Lifeboat Institution Coxswain Leng and the crew of the lifeboat received special awards for gallantry.

The Northern Crown

Wrecked off the coast of Iceland in October 1956, and with their lifeboats washed away, the 20-man crew of the Grimsby trawler *Northern Crown* had only inflatable rafts to carry them to safety. But the flimsy craft did the trick and, aided by the Icelandic gunboat *Thor*, all the men survived the ordeal. The *Northern Crown* was the fourth Humberside trawler that year to be lost without the loss of life. And altogether 57 men had been saved by rubber dinghies. The other ships lost were the *Osako* and *Jane Jorgensen* from Grimsby and the *St Cellestin* of Hull.

Stricken

It was at 6.45 am that the *Northern Crown*'s SOS was picked up in Iceland. She had stranded in heavy seas on the rocky islet of Eldey, which rises out of the sea to a height of 226ft, eight miles south-west of Reykjanes Point off Iceland's south-west coast. Once the Mayday call was received the gunboat *Thor* was guided to the trawler by an American aircraft which flew from Iceland. When the *Thor* arrived at 9.20 am the stricken trawler was in bad shape. The engine room had been completely flooded by 8 am and just 30 minutes later the two life-boats were washed overboard. During the night the weather had been atrocious. A south-westerly gale had been blowing and although the weather moderated somewhat during the early morning it was still bad when the *Thor* arrived. Once on the scene *Thor* advised Skipper Colin Newton to get the crew into the self-inflating dinghies. This was quickly done and the *Thor* picked up the first dinghy and then the other, saving the whole of the crew by about 10 am — just a little over three hours after the vessel had gone ashore.

Very soon after the rescue the thanks of the Grimsby people were sent to the trawler's Icelandic agent Mr Geir Zoega by the secretary of the Grimsby Steam Fishing Vessels Mutual Insurance and Protecting Co Ltd, Mr J V Chatburn.

Holidays

Skipper Newton was acting as relief skipper of the *Northern Crown*. Her regular skipper, Mr August Ebernezersson, had taken two trips off as a holiday. As the *Thor* left the scene with the rescued crewmen aboard the *Northern Crown* was gradually disappearing beneath the grey, turbulent sea. And 24 hours later reports reached Grimsby that the vessel was a total loss. She had sunk in 60 fathoms of water. The crewmen were landed at Reykjavik and were soon on their way home. It was only then that the full story of the dramatic events and of the heroism of one man became clear. He was chief engineer Mr A E Horsley, who lived in Daubney Street, Cleethorpes. His 19 colleagues claimed he had done "what only one man in 1,000 would have done" and saved their lives.

Burners

A modest Mr Horsley told an *Evening Telegraph* reporter at the time how he had been on watch when the trawler hit the rocks. He switched off the three burners as the engine room rapidly filled with oil and water and he

16. The Northern Crown, new in 1953 and lost within three years.

realised the ship was in grave danger.

"The skipper rang down for me to go astern and my second, Mr A Letch, managed to pull the lever over. The skipper then rang down for us to go ahead. With a little bit of trouble I managed to manipulate the stop valve," he said. But that action almost certainly saved the trawler from hitting the rocks again. Fireman Mr Frank Mitchell of Cleethorpes went so far as to declare of Mr Horsley: "If it had not been for him I don't think we would have been here now." He claimed that with the engine room flooded to a depth of four feet Mr Horsley turned the trawler ahead after she struck the reef.

"To do that he had to lie down almost on top of the oil with one hand clutching a rail and the other trying to turn the wheel. This by some miracle he managed to do. I think only one man in 1,000 would have attempted to do what our chief engineer did," he told the reporter.

Even when the men had got themselves aboard the inflatables their problems were not over. Once over the side the dinghies began to drift alongside and very close to the crippled trawler. With a lot of planking hanging down from the damaged vessel there was a danger of it splitting the rubber boats. Frantically the crew pushed themselves away from the trawler and eventually got free of her. One of the dinghies overturned as the men were boarding her. Deckhands Douglas Stoneman and John Andrews of Grimsby were trapped inside the overturned inflatable. Other men, who had been thrown into the water, quickly righted the dinghy.

Glowing

All the survivors had glowing praise for the inflatables which in those days cost in the region of £200. Douglas Stoneman, who was just 17 at the time, said on his arrival home: "If it had not been for the dinghies we would all have been goners."

In June 1957 Grimsby extended its thanks for the services rendered by the Icelanders and the United States Air Sea Rescue Service in Iceland. An inscribed silver cigarette box was presented to Capt Eirikur Kristofersson, captain of the *Thor*. The Icelandic Life Saving Association also got a cheque for £300. A reception in Iceland was attended by Capt Kristofersson and 25 other members of the crew. Also there were representatives of Reykjavik Radio, the crew of the American Skymaster aircraft which led the search, the crew of the motor boat *Muninn*, which also joined in the search and officials of other rescue organisations.

The full crew of the *Northern Crown* on that fateful trip was: Skipper Newton; mate Roy McDonald; third hand W H Roberts; chief engineer A E Horsley; second engineer A Letch; firemen G Goddard, F Mitchell; deckhand/trimmers C R Germaney, C Thomas; cook A Pye; galley boy R E Starr; deckhands A Gambrell, J Andrews, E Pavell, L Standley, L Capes, K Chapman, E Phillipson; deckhand/learner D Stoneman; radio operator I Griffith.

Launched

One fisherman had a case of anthrax to thank for not being aboard for the trawler's final trip. Mr Charles Kurz senior, of Hainton Avenue, Grimsby, was regular third hand on the trawler, having joined her when she was new. He recalled: "I fortunately wasn't on board. I went down to sail at tide time feeling a bit groggy. My eyes had been smarting for the previous couple of days and the Skipper looked at me and sent me straight to the doctors. I'd got anthrax in both eyes. It was caught from the cow hides we used in the cod ends. I first learned of the tragic loss of the *Crown* when my daughter-in-law told me she had been lost."

The *Northern Crown* was launched on 17 March 1953 at the Selby yard of Cochrane and Sons Ltd. Her name was taken from one of the Coronation emblems.

She was the first new trawler built for Grimsby owners since the war to

SALMON CUTLETS

Tin of salmon with oil poured away, add a little salt, pepper and ground mace, 2 ozs. breadcrumbs and a little egg to bind the mixture. Take away all the bones from the fish, soak the breadcrumbs in about 2 tablespoonfuls of milk, then add them to the salmon along with the seasoning and eggs. Make up into cutlets, brush over with egg, cover with breadcrumbs and fry in boiling fat. When cooked place a piece of macaroni in the end of each and dish up in a circle. Serve either hot or cold.

make use of coal as fuel. The trawler was some 180ft long and 750 gross tons. Reports at the time of her launch spoke of innovations in her crew accommodations. The mate and the chief engineer had their cabins in the main bridge structure. Skipper August Ebernezersson commanded the trawler on her maiden voyage. Early in 1955 the trawler made the news when she collided with the isolated "bullnose" of the west pier of the Royal Dock Basin in Grimsby. The "bullnose", which bore a battery-operated flashing light, was tipped over. The *Northern Crown* suffered damage to her propoller. However, she was able to dock and landed her 1,200 Iceland kits.

Just a few weeks later the trawler was in the public eye again for a very different reason. Skipper Ebernezersson and the rest of the crew were interviewed by a team from the BBC in Manchester about the effects of black frost.

The *Northern Crown* had been in contact with the killer-ice for about a week before she returned from the fishing grounds to Grimsby. The interview was later transmitted on *Television Newsreel*. But only 18 months later the trawler sailed her last trip, ending her days on that bleak, inhospitable rocky coast.

The Osako

Three months after seeing a demonstration of life-saving dinghies in the docks, a local skipper found himself launching them to save the crew of the Grimsby trawler *Osako*.

Off the Faroes the *Osako* had sprung a leak and was rapidly filling with water. It was 21 April 1956. Skipper Harry Ellis, of another Grimsby vessel, the *Thessalonian*, was listening to his radio as the gale-lashed seas tossed the trawler around. Suddenly the message came that the *Osako*'s fish room was leaking and the pumps were unable to cope with the inrush of water. It became clear that the vessel would not be able to stay afloat for long. The *Thessalonian*, launched only the year before, immediately responded and headed for the scene. When she reached the scene Skipper Ellis realised he could not get up close because of the state of the sea. But his vessel had become the first to be equipped with the dinghies. And, although he had no practical experience in using them, Skipper Ellis decided he had to try.

Shuttle

The crew of the *Osako* were desperately clinging to the rails of their ship as Skipper Ellis floated the dinghies on a line to the stricken vessel. For two hours they were hauled back and forth in a dramatic shuttle service until the 13 men of the *Osako* were all safely aboard the *Thessalonian*. Last to leave the sinking trawler was her skipper, Mr Harold Gladwell. He tried until the end to save his ship. Desperately he secured a towline, but it had to be cut as the *Osako* continued to sink deeper into the water. The *Thessalonian* then steamed for Thorshavn, capital of the Faroes, to land the rescued men, some of whom were suffering from cold and exposure. They were all taken to hospital for a check-up.

17, 18. ***below and overleaf:*** *The rescuers. Crew members of the Grimsby trawler Thessalonian which rescued the crew of the Osako.*

When they arrived back in Grimsby, Skipper Gladwell told how the men had joked as they abandoned ship and jumped into the dinghies. He told how, when the *Osako* started leaking, he had tried to call other vessels operated by the same owners, Taylor's, but the *Thessalonian*, a Sir Thomas Robinson ship, had answered. The *Osako*'s crew had tried to find the leak in the fish room but it got worse and worse, becoming more than the crew could cope with. They had tried bailing with buckets but the water had gradually got the better of them.

19. *The replacement Osako launched in 1958.*

Fine Job

Then the *Thessalonian* arrived on the scene with her dinghies. Skipper Gladwell told the *Evening Telegraph* at the time: "Her skipper did a fine job of work. I sent seven of the men off in the larger dinghy. They had seen the way the dinghies had behaved in the water, and had not the slightest hesitation in jumping in. They joked about it, their morale being splendid. We all knew we had nothing to worry about, no matter what the weather was like.

"If we had not had the dinghies we should have had to try to launch our boat. In the seas that were running and with the way the *Osako* was rolling we would have been very lucky to have done it without accident. These liferafts are a great thing." Skipper Gladwell said that everyone had to leave the *Osako* in the end and six men had crowded into the smaller dinghy.

The full crew of the *Osako* was: Skipper H L G Gladwell; mate H Burgess; third hand C Taylor; first engineer V Brown; second engineer G A Bennett; deckhands P Brennan, H Sheldrick, C Pitchers; trimmers F Marris, C Dickie; firemen T Hood, E Yenney; cook R Smith. Skipper Ellis of the *Thessalonian* was full of praise for the dinghies, too. After the drama of the rescue he said: "Without the dinghies it would have been a dangerous job. If I had not had them I would have tried to launch my boat, but it might have smashed against the ship's side." He also told how he always left his radio switched on and how he had heard the *Osako*'s call for help.

The *Thessalonian* had been only five or six miles away and was alongside the *Osako* in 15 minutes. Twice Skipper Ellis fired line-carrying rockets over the trawler, but the strong winds carried both lines away. It was then he brought the new dinghies into use.

Not long afterwards the *Osako* took a heavy list to starboard and sank about 12 hours after sending her first distress call. In the 12 hours they had made about 20 miles towards the Faroes. Skipper Ellis said: "In my opinion the *Osako* men owed their lives in some measure to the fact that my ship carried dinghies. We have always had them, one for 10 men and one for six. They were put on board when the *Thessalonian* was new, and we were given training in their use."

Mr Goodman, one of the deckhands who tried to get a line to the *Osako*, told the *Evening Telegraph* at the time that he thought the dinghies were marvellous. "There was no danger in it at all. The dinghy rode over the waves and was quite level," he said.

The then secretary of the Grimsby Trawler Officers Guild, Capt E J Beaumont, said the dinghies had proved immensely valuable in saving life at sea. The *Osako* was quickly replaced with another vessel of the same name. She sailed on her first trip in November 1958, and fished until only a few years ago, when she became another victim of the decline in the fishing industry. She was eventually sold to a foreign company which intended to send her prawn-fishing.

The Revello

At midday on 7 December 1959 the Grimsby trawler *Revello*, battered by North Sea gales, sank beneath the waves. The 11-man crew, realising their predicament, took to their liferafts and all were saved. But in another drama the 12-man crew of the Aberdeen trawler *George Robb* were lost when the ship went ashore near Duncansbay Head, Caithness in the wild weather.

The *Revello* had been built in Beverley in 1908. She was 107 net tons in weight. She sank off Spurn Point. The lucky crew were rescued by the 7,000 ton Newcastle steamer *Baluchistan*.

20. Skipper Robinson looking thoughtful as he sits in the bus which took the men home.

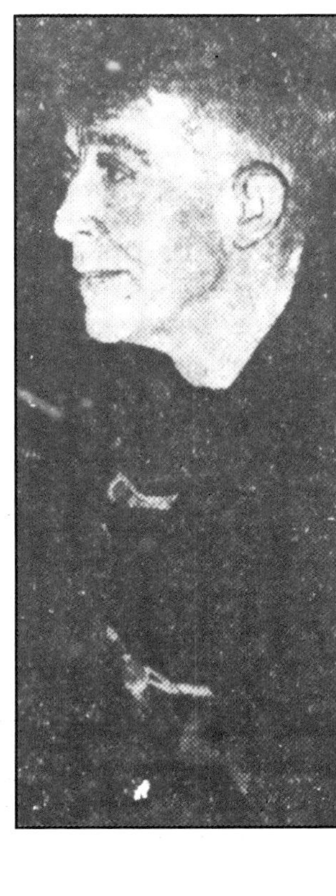

Before they were landed safely at Immingham later the same day they told the *Evening Telegraph* over the radio about their dramatic escape. The *Revello*'s skipper, Mr J C Robinson, who lived in Miller Avenue, Grimsby, and the captain of the steamer, B S J de Neumann, pieced together the details of the rescue which occurred 18 miles off Spurn. The first message from Capt de Neumann said:

"Conditions are still very bad but we have all the *Revello*'s 11 men on board and they are all OK.

"They had already abandoned their ship when we saw them and were in their inflated liferafts. The weather was terrible but they drifted towards us." He told a reporter that the rescue was rather difficult but only to be expected in the shocking weather conditions they were experiencing. And he stressed: "The great thing is that the crew are all right."

Lucky

Shortly after being picked up Skipper Robinson said he was still shivering with cold. He told what happened.

"We sprang a leak and the water came in so fast that the pumps could not cope with it. We had to abandon the ship. It is lucky the *Baluchistan* was there. We were very grateful to them. We are all fine." He said the vessel had had a lovely trip but the weather had been atrocious on the way back to port. The *Revello* had been due in Grimsby on the morning tide. She stayed afloat for three and a half hours after being abandoned. Another Grimsby trawler, the *Rizzio*, which had the same owners as the *Revello* — Ross Trawlers Ltd — also answered the vessel's distress call.

The *Revello* had left for the North Sea fishing grounds just a week before. There were sighs of relief amongst the families of the *Revello*'s crew when they

21. Trimmer W Oxley (left) of Tiverton Street, Cleethorpes and deckhand A Pedersen arrive ashore in borrowed clothing after surviving the sinking of the Revello.

learned their men were safe. Skipper Robinson's wife explained at the time that he was a stand-in for the regular skipper, Mr E Bennett, who had been taken ill on the last trip. She told the *Evening Telegraph*:

"My husband did not intend to go to sea until after Christmas but agreed to this one trip in the *Revello*." The youngest member of the crew was 16-year-old Robert Elliott, who lived in Bridge Street, Grimsby. He was making his first North Sea trip — against his mother's advice. She told a *Telegraph* reporter: "I did not want him to go in one of those North Sea ships." He had been fishing deep sea trawlers since leaving school a year before. He had always sailed as galley boy before but on that occasion went as a deckie-learner.

Lost All

Other members of the crew included third hand L Baxter, of Park Street, Cleethorpes; second engineer J Tyas, Marcus Street, Grimsby; deckhands A Pedersen, Dolphin Street, Cleethorpes and R H Perin, Lovett Street, Cleethorpes; trimmers W Poll, Guildford Street, Grimsby and W Oxley, Tiverton Street, Cleethorpes: and cook Mr A Hamilton, Barcroft Street, Cleethorpes. On arrival at Immingham the survivors told more about the drama. Skipper Robinson said to waiting *Evening Telegraph* reporters: "We've lost everything. I even lost this year's Christmas present from my wife — an electric razor."

The rain was still lashing down and a gale force wind was blowing as the tug *Lady Sarah* took the men off the steamer *Baluchistan*. They were all wearing clothing borrowed from the crew of the Newcastle ship. Skipper Robinson paid further credit to Capt de Neumann and the crew of the *Baluchistan*. He said: "They were wonderful to us. We cannot thank them enough."

The chief engineer, Mr G Cressey, told the *Evening Telegraph*: "We sprang a leak about 2.34 am. It was just a trickle at first but I soon found that I was almost up to my waist in water in the engine room. I tried to stem it but it was impossible." He said the order to abandon ship had been given around 6.45 am. In 25 years at sea it was his first shipwreck. Trimmer Mr W Poll was the only man who fell in the sea.

Slipped

He explained at the time: "I slipped as I was going aboard the steamer. But I grabbed hold of the ropes and was hauled up to the ship." Second engineer Mr Tyas said the men had been in the dinghies about two to three hours before being picked up. He said:

"Before we left the *Revello* the water was up to my knees." Young Elliott told a reporter that he had been awakened about six o' clock and told that the ship was sinking. "We got into a raft and then we were picked up by the steamer. This has not put me off the sea. I shall go back." he said. The cook, Mr A Hamilton, was celebrating his birthday when the ship went down. "A fine way of celebrating," he said.

Mr John R Cobb, of Corporation Road, Grimsby, was third hand on the *Rizzio* at the time of the sinking. And he vividly recalled what happened.

"I was called out from watch below to stow the fishing gear on board as the *Revello* was taking in water from a hole below the boiler.

"It was blowing quite hard and we steamed full out to her assistance. We arrived about 9.30 to 10 am to find that her crew had been taken from a liferaft on board a steamer. Everyone was OK and no one was injured," he said.

The *Rizzio* stood by the *Revello* and the weather gradually abated. "The mate and myself offered to board the *Revello* to see if it was possible to take her in tow. The office indicated that no risks should be taken. "The skipper stayed with me on watch as we stood off close by. The *Revello* was getting heavy and rolling sluggishly in the water.

Disaster !

The Leicestershire

In a corner of Scartho Cemetery, Grimsby, stands a memorial dedicated to the memory of 15 men who lost their lives when the trawler *Leicestershire* was overwhelmed by a gale in the Orkneys. It was one of the worst tragedies ever to hit Grimsby's fishing fleet. And it was particularly sad because the vessel was on her way home when disaster struck in January 1938. Just one crewman survived. Galleyboy J Willett, who lived in Stirling Street, Grimsby, was taken ill while the vessel was fishing off Iceland and was taken into hospital with appendicitis.

The first news to reach Grimsby came in a report which said that bodies and wreckage had been washed on the island of Hoy in the Orkneys. Part of the trawler's boat was picked up bearing the word Grimsby and part of a wireless set was also found with the mark No 1125. There was a maker's name on the fragment of boat which made it clear it had come from a trawler built by Smith's Dock Company and that narrowed down the inquiry to firms which had ships of that class.

Early on 31 January 1938 it became clear that the missing ship was the *Leicestershire*, owned by the Leicestershire Steam Fishing Company and managed by H Markham Cook Ltd, who operated the County class of trawlers. The *Leicestershire* had been on a fishing trip to Iceland and was homeward bound with her catch. She was due in Grimsby on 31 January. She had spoken to another Grimsby vessel, the *Northern Chief*, on 27 January when she was 40 miles from The Skerries. Shortly afterwards Wick Radio had a message from the trawler which put her position as 30 miles from The Skerries. That was the last news from the vessel until the wreckage was found.

22. The Leicestershire.

Twelve Married

There were reports of appalling gales in the North Atlantic during the week and on Friday, 28 January there was one in particular which was extremely violent. The feeling was that the *Leicestershire* had been caught in it and eventually overwhelmed by its ferocity. Of the 15 men who died 12 were married. No fewer than 23 children were left fatherless.

The crew was: Skipper Alfred Evans, of Park Street, Grimsby; mate G Neslin, Grafton Street, Grimsby; first engineer C Slater, Kathleen Avenue, Cleethorpes; second engineer R Holloway, Bentley Street, Cleethorpes; third engineer A Booth, Escart Avenue, Grimsby; deckhands W Revell, Cromwell Road, Grimsby, H Byrom, Grove Crescent, Grimsby, J Connelly, Albert Street, Grimsby, H Miller, Johnson Street, Cleethorpes, T Burkitt, Willingham Street, Grimsby, A Miller, Sussex Street, Cleethorpes; steward A Blyth, Grimsby Road, Cleethorpes; firemen H Symonds, Tunnard Street, Grimsby, H Lancaster, King Edward Street, Grimsby; radio operator R C Moreland, Legsby Avenue, Grimsby.

Skipper Evans was 25 and a member of one of the port's best known fishing families. He had been a skipper for five years but this was his first trip in the *Leicestershire*. Formerly he had skippered the *Northern Chief*, the trawler which, by a strange coincidence, was the last vessel to be in touch with the *Leicestershire*. Reports from Orkney said the naked body of one man had been washed ashore on Saturday, 29 January. Three more bodies were washed ashore on Sunday and a fourth could be seen tossing about in the breakers.

Searchers led by William Ross, Frank Meiklejohn, John Ross and William Buchan, all of Melsetter, searched the coast from Torness to Berry in snow and hail on Sunday, 30 January and managed to recover the bodies which had been washed ashore. As the days passed more bodies were washed ashore. More wreckage, including part of a Marconi radio set, also came ashore. That turned the fears of a disaster into reality because it was established that particular radio had been issued to the *Leicestershire* in 1936 when she was new.

Towns Stunned

Taking into account the last radio message received from the *Leicestershire* it was estimated that she must have gone ashore near Torness Head on the island of Hoy which is on the northern shore and the westerly entrance to the Pentland Firth. With the whole of Grimsby and Cleethorpes stunned and in mourning the Red Ensign flew at half mast outside the office of H Markham

23. Coffins of some of the Leicestershire victims lying in state at the Fishermen's Bethel Mission in Tiverton Street, Cleethorpes.

24. ***left***: *The first of the bodies of the Leicestershire crew are carried ashore. Among the bearers was Skipper Alfred Evans, whose son was the skipper of the ill-fated trawler.*
25. ***below:*** *A family bereaved: Mrs Miller of Sussex Street, Cleethorpes and her three children left fatherless by the Leicestershire disaster.*

Cook on the Fish Docks. The Grimsby trawler *Pembroke Castle* had reported she was some 60 miles behind the *Leicestershire* on the way home. The anxiety for the safety of the *Leicestershire* had increased when the *Pembroke Castle* arrived in Grimsby only to find the other vessel had not appeared. Port Missioner Mr H Pickering had the unenviable task of going to the homes of the relatives of the missing men and breaking the tragic news.

Meanwhile in the Orkneys attempts continued to identify the bodies which had been washed ashore. Descriptions of tattoos and other identifying features were sent back to Grimsby. One body had a tattoo of a dagger and a snake, another had the tip of the forefinger of the right hand missing.

The Port Missioner had just conducted a memorial service for seven Grimsby seamen killed in Tarragona, Spain, by Franco's bombs which struck the vessel the *Thorpeness*. But suddenly he was faced with organising yet another.Meanwhile news was coming through from the Orkneys of the heroism of the islanders who ran considerable risks to recover the bodies of the fishermen. Relatives were concerned at news that one body had been sighted but could not be recovered. It was lying on a ledge under a high overhanging cliff in a position where it was hidden from the islanders who were searching the area.

Too High

However, it was eventually seen from a point further down the coast and steps were taken to try to recover it. The first idea was to lower a man on a rope but it was realised that the man would not be able to swing himself far enough in to reach the ledge. The ledge was too high above high water marks for there to be any hope of reaching it by boat. The islanders had to wait for several days until a low tide enabled them to make a further attempt. Further along the coast the rescue party descended the cliff and clambered over the rocks.

Then followed a dangerous climb until they finally reached the ledge where the body had been seen. It was lowered carefully from ledge to ledge and carried over the rocks, along the foot of the cliffs to a spot where the party could scale the towering rockface. Eventually the rescue party reached the nearest road, a considerable distance from the cliff top. Sadly, the body was not identified and it was finally laid to rest in the Orkneys. The bodies of the two other crewmen which had been so badly battered by the sea as to be unidentifiable were also buried in the Orkneys. Six other men were brought home to Grimsby for a joint burial service.

Sad Cargoes Put Town in Mourning

February 1938 was not yet a week old when the trawler *Hampshire* hove into sight off the Humber bearing the saddest cargo she would ever carry. Six coffins lay on deck, curious black coffins like they make in the Orkneys, and each contained a member of the crew of the ill-fated *Leicestershire* which had foundered with the loss of all hands just a few days previously. It was Sunday night, 6 February and with the co-operation of other ships also in the river the *Hampshire* wound her way forward to take up a leading position. She would be first through the LocPit gates. Ashore, with lumps in their throats and tears in their eyes, friends and relatives peered through the gloom and caught sight of the *Hampshire*'s deck lights gleaming across the dark water. There was a berth reserved for her when she finally came in, her arrival watched in silence by hundreds. Harry Markham Cook, for the owners, the Lincolnshire Steam Fishing Company, was first aboard and in the nearby streets, hearses were marshalled and arranged.

The *Leicestershire*'s skipper, Alfred Evans, came of one of Grimsby's best known fishing families and five of his relatives led by his father — also a skipper and also called Alfred — strode aboard and began the unloading of the dead.

Cortege Set Off

The cortege set off down Fish Dock Road, quiet now, for it was a Sunday evening, and past hundreds gathered at the Fish Dock Road level crossing and clustered at Riby Square. Sadly and slowly they made their way to the Tiverton Street Bethel Mission, the fishermen's own chapel, and their burdens were borne within. The following day, and after relatives had made their pilgrimage, the public in their hundreds poured through to pay their last respects. Wreaths arrived, small ones, spectacular ones, some shaped like trawlers, one as a colossal anchor. Grimsby was a town in deep mourning.

Tuesday, 8 February dawned grey and overcast. It was bitterly cold. But all over the town people were bracing themselves for the harrowing funeral to come. Sir Walter and Lady Womersley, the Mayors of Grimsby and Cleethorpes, the trawler's owners, members of the Grimsby Trawler Officers' Guild, friends, colleagues — and their relatives, 12 widows and 23 children — had one final duty to perform.

26, 27. ***below and opposite page:*** *The Grimsby's cemetery memorial to the Leicestershire's crew.*

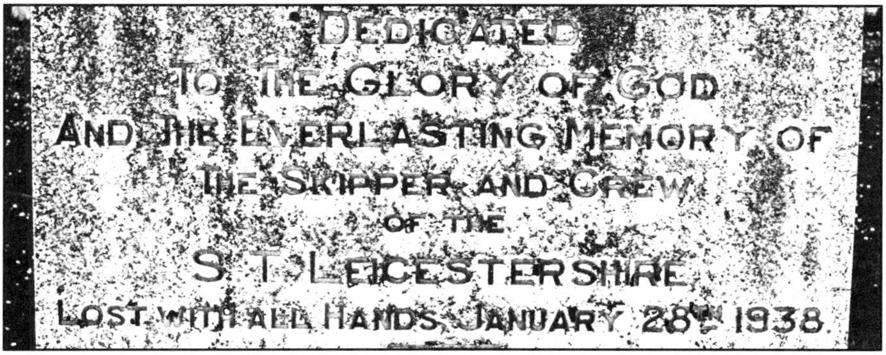

The Port Missioner, Mr Harold Pickering, conducted a moving but simple service, steadying his congregation, alleviating their grief. It took 40 minutes for duty to be done, for respect to be paid, for the community to be reminded of its joint sorrow.

Great Risks

The coffins were taken outside for their final journey. The sinking of the *Leicestershire* had moved not only Grimsby but the nation. Almost at the same time Fleetwood was plunged into despair over the disappearance of the *Bostonian*. Every man in England was suddenly aware of the appalling risks taken that he might enjoy a fish supper.

"Little do we know of the hardships that these brave fellows undergo . . . and still less can we appreciate their trials in the trouble that has just been experienced," wrote an official of an orphanage.

Tiverton Street was thronged with mourners. One end was totally blocked by them. Six deep they stood, along Grimsby Road and along Cleethorpe Road and along Freeman Street.

The cortege, six hearses and twice as many black saloons, moved at snail's pace. Down Hainton Avenue, past curtained windows and on to Weelsby Road it wound, the kerbs a platform for silent people, bare-headed, some weeping, and so to Scartho Road Cemetery. The journey took an hour. Six graves, in line, awaited the six coffins in their six hearses. And by their side stood the Port Missioner, his final act to do, a last gesture to write "finis" at the foot of yet another Grimsby disaster.

Of course there were more than six on the *Leicestershire* when she foundered. But the sea had not released all its dead and some had been too disfigured to allow for identification. Those found soon after the tragedy, and then subsequently, lie in the Orkneys yet, beneath a nine-foot memorial like the one at Scartho that bears the names of ALL the crew.

Although sympathy to all involved was given unstintingly, there was ample room for substantial assistance. Mr George Tickler raised a spontaneous £25 from members of the Grimsby and Cleethorpes Unionist Association. And he was not alone in his generosity. Already burdened by a staggering 145 losses in the previous five years, the Grimsby Fishermen's Dependents' Fund rallied to the call for help, committing themselves to a further paying out of £2,900 over the following five-year period. The Mayor's Fund was again drawn upon, as was the *Evening Telegraph*'s similar charity.

It was less than a fortnight later that the name of the steam trawler *Leicestershire* once more found its place in the headlines in Grimsby. For, in the distant Orkneys, lobster fishermen from Longhope, maybe some of the very men who helped to recover the *Leicestershire*'s grim cargo, sighted a ship off a submerged rock known locally as The Tift. They found her at low tide 50 yards from steep cliffs, on her side, holed.

It was indeed the *Leicestershire*. She had sunk immediately and her crew had had neither chance to lower a boat or struggle ashore in the storm tossed sea.

The Moravia

28. The damaged Moravia arriving in Grimsby with flag at half mast.

Badly battered, her funnel and mizzen mast missing, wheelhouse smashed and ventilator and rails twisted, the Grimsby trawler *Moravia* was towed into port late on 17 April 1932. The vessel had been severely damaged when she was struck by mountainous seas while operating in Icelandic waters. Tragically her skipper, Mr Jack Fradley, and a deckhand, Mr George William Pratt, both lost their lives in the incident. And as the *Moravia* came back to Grimsby the red ensign flew at half-mast as a tribute to the two men.

First news of the disaster came on 11 April when a radio message reported the trawler had been cleanswept in the gale. The message was passed to the vessel's owners, the Great Grimsby and East Coast Steam Fishing Company, by Skipper Hall of the trawler *Embassy*, also a Grimsby vessel. It read: "*Moravia* being towed, lost funnel, bridge, mizzen mast; severely damaged. Also lost Skipper Fradley and deckhand Pratt. Now 130 miles south east of Westmann Islands. *Cape Grisnez* towing." The *Cape Grisnez* was a Hull trawler, owned by the Hudson Steam Fishing Company.

It was on 24 March 1932 that the *Moravia* left Grimsby for the Icelandic fishing grounds. She carried 12 men. But it was not until the trawler finally arrived back in port that the full story of the tragedy emerged. It was only a few hours after the *Moravia* had left the fishing grounds that the battering came. A wave struck the trawler broadside and carried the skipper and deckhand Pratt overboard with part of the wheelhouse. The battering left the ship helpless. She drifted broadside before the gale for 36 hours before her signals of distress were answered by the *Cape Grisnez*. When she arrived on the scene her crewmen's first impression of the sea-swept trawler was that it was a ship upside down. By very skilful seamanship the skipper of the Hull trawler came alongside the *Moravia* and took her in tow. Then in the teeth of a fierce gale the *Cape Grisnez* hung on to the crippled trawler. On five occasions the tow rope parted in the treacherous conditions but the operation went on. Eventually the *Moravia* was towed back to the comparative safety of the Humber — a distance of some 900 miles.

The *Cape Grisnez* had been one of the last ships the *Moravia* had spoken to before leaving the fishing grounds on the west side of Iceland to go to those on the east side.

Survivors

Skipper Chapman of the *Cape Grisnez* spoke to Skipper Fradley and told him they had lost some of their fishing gear. Skipper Fradley replied: "It's the luck of the game, boy." When the *Cape Grisnez* answered the *Moravia*'s call for help and Skipper Chapman learned that Skipper Fradley had been lost he repeated, sadly: "It's the luck of the game, boy."

The survivors from the *Moravia* were: Mate Mr W Hopwood; first engineer Mr A T East; second engineer Mr W Farrington; third hand Mr E J F Firth; deckhands Mr J Mudd, Mr M Pearce, Mr W S Hodgson, Mr A A Robinson, Mr H Murry; and cook Mr F Best.

When the two men were lost overboard the only other man on watch was the third hand Mr Edward Firth who had a narrow escape from death. When the trawler docked he told an *Evening Telegraph* reporter of his experiences.

Weather

"Everything went well and we completed our trip by 10.30 on the morning of 9 April, and we started for home. The weather was bad at the time with a strong gale blowing from east-north-east.

"Shortly before 6 pm on 9 April I was on watch in the wheelhouse with deckhand Pratt and the Skipper. Owing to the bad weather everything was battened down.

"We saw a big sea rolling up on the port side and just before it reached the ship I crouched down in the front part of the wheelhouse and the skipper and Pratt, who was at the wheel, stepped back.

"The sea struck us almost broadside and the ship heeled over to starboard.

"As the water cleared I heard the whistle blowing and I thought the skipper was giving a signal for one reason or other.

"Then I noticed that the companion and the back of the wheelhouse had gone and that the top of the funnel had disappeared.

"The lower half of the funnel was twisted and the steam pipe was bent right down with the whistle still blowing."

Mr Firth told how the force of the sea caused the ship to heel over and how her starboard rail was under water.

"If she had taken a second sea she would certainly have never come up again. It was nearly a quarter of an hour before the ship got on anything like an even keel.

"When I realised what had happened I went to the wheel and tried to get the head of the ship to the wind, but I found that this was impossible.

"By this time the mate came on deck and inquired where the skipper was and I told him I thought he had gone on deck. I did not realise that he had been washed overboard.

"We tried to keep the head of the ship to the wind by putting out a sea anchor but this method failed because there was no steam pressure.

Distress

"So we hoisted a signal of distress and hoped for the best.

"Thirty-six hours elapsed before we sighted another ship and all the time we were drifting broadside before the wind.

"Eventually the *Cape Grisnez* came up and when she got within hailing distance her skipper said he thought at first that the *Moravia* was a ship upside down.

"The *Cape Grisnez* got hold of us, the skipper navigating close enough to us to throw a line on board," Mr Firth told the reporter.

The weather had remained bad until the two ships got off the east coast of Scotland, then it improved.

"It was not until later that we realised the extent of the damage, for in addition to the wheelhouse being wrecked and the funnel swept away, the ventilators were twisted, the mizzen mast was carried away and the small boat was smashed to pieces," said Mr Firth. Chief engineer Mr Alfred East, who lived in Stanley Street, Grimsby, was on watch in the engine room at the time the sea struck the *Moravia*.

29. Crew members of the Moravia after their trawler had been towed home after being battered in a storm in which the skipper and a deckhand were drowned.

Overboard

He was surprised to hear the whistle blowing. Deciding to investigate he went to the speaking tube. However, when he removed the plug, water poured out of the tube. The engine room then began to fill up with smoke and steam. Mr East ran on deck where he met the mate who told him he believed the skipper had gone overboard. Realising what had happened the chief engineer went below and, feeling his way through a cloud of steam, reached the top of the boiler where he turned off the steam that was passing through the pipe to the whistle.

One of the deckhands, Mr Matt Pearce, who rushed into the engine room to give assistance, had his arm badly scalded by the escaping steam. The mate, Mr William Hopwood, who lived in Clee Road, and who took command after the loss of the skipper, told reporters he arrived on deck practically as the damage was done. Speaking at the time he said: "I made my way up to what was left of the bridge and found the third hand had got the ship's head to wind.

"But we found it impossible to keep the ship's head to the wind as she was losing steam all the time. I asked the third hand where the skipper was and he said he thought he had gone on deck.

"I realised, however, that he might have been washed overboard and made certain by searching the ship and finding no trace of him."

At the time of the tragedy the *Moravia* had been 48 miles south east by south of Ingoldshuf on the east coast of Iceland. The state of the sea made it impossible to see any object from the trawler. Because of the crippled state of the *Moravia* and the shocking weather there was no attempt to take the survivors off the vessel.

Although the *Moravia* was repaired and returned to sea she was eventually to meet a sticky end, for she was blown up by a mine while on active service in the North Sea in the spring of 1943.

The Janet Helen

Magnificent seamanship by a Grimsby skipper enabled a trawler to manoeuvre alongside the sinking "baby" trawler *Janet Helen* and get a line aboard. As the 73-foot vessel sank, the trawler *War Duke* — also from Grimsby — managed to get to it and put two men aboard with a line. The action brought loud praise for the *War Duke*'s skipper, Mr George Ireland. But the valiant effort could not save the *Janet Helen* which, battered by the gales and heavy seas, finally sank.

Only two years old when she was lost, the *Janet Helen* had been heralded as one way of solving the problem of the future of North Sea fishing from the port — mainly because of her ability to fish the whole year round. But ironically it was the stormy winter weather which was finally to see the end of the vessel.

Fight Fails

It was on 10 December 1959 that the *Evening Telegraph* gave the news of the vessel's demise. A dramatic fight to try to save the trawler — the only "baby" one in the port — had failed after the five-man crew had been forced to abandon her in a gale 30 miles south-east of Flamborough Head.

The drama began when the *Janet Helen* sprang a leak in the engine room which flooded to a depth of three feet as the pumps were unable to cope. After around 15 minutes in a dinghy the five men aboard were picked up by the *War Duke* which had answered the radio call for help. Later the *Janet Helen*'s skipper, Mr Ernest Neal, who lived in Wellington Street, Grimsby, and the mate, Mr Brian Walker, who lived next door, re-boarded the vessel to fix a tow rope and were taken off again. Then the problem of towing the vessel, hampered by the gale, began. The line parted but another was got on board.

After several hours with the *War Duke* only managing two knots, a heavy sea struck the *Janet Helen* and she went down stern first about 14 miles from Spurn Point. The *War Duke* held her with the 75-fathom warp until she settled on the bottom, when the line was chopped away. The trawler then headed for Grimsby with the five-man crew of the "baby" vessel aboard.

It was about 4.45 am on 10 December 1959 that the leak developed in the *Janet Helen*'s engine room. The crew were unable to locate it and when the pumps could not cope radio contact was established with the *War Duke* around 4.58 am. At 5.20 am the *War Duke* reported she was only about 10 minutes' steaming away from the "baby" trawler. But three minutes later when the water in the engine room was three feet deep Skipper Neal gave the order to abandon ship. The crew left in the rubber dinghy.

Clear Story

But it was only when the men returned to Grimsby that the full story of the rescue became clear. In spite of the towering waves whipped up by the wind Skipper Ireland of the *War Duke* was able to hold the vessel long enough to allow the skipper and mate of the *Janet Helen* to jump back aboard their slowly sinking ship to fix a tow rope.

Tribute to the seamanship of Skipper Ireland and his crew was paid by the *Janet Helen* crewmen when they reached home. Skipper Neal told waiting reporters: "It was a wonderful piece of work." The *Janet Helen* had been towed around 13 miles when she finally sank beneath the waves.

Skipper Ireland said: "We kept the tow rope on until the last minute. It seemed as if she did not want to go — her bows stuck up in the water for about half an hour." He said they had been fishing about two miles away when they received the *Janet Helen* distress call.

"It did not take us much longer than 20 minutes to steam to her," he said.

Skipper Ireland played down the difficulty of actually taking the men on board his vessel. It was the first time he had experienced inflatable dinghies and he described them as "wonderful things". He told how twice the *Janet Helen*'s skipper and mate had gone back aboard the stricken vessel. The second time they were able to fix the rope.

"The decks were awash all the time. We were disappointed to see the ship go after all that but the main thing was that the men were safe," said Skipper Ireland.

Skipper Ireland had been going to sea for 22 years at the time of the incident. He lived in Braemar Road, Cleethorpes. Both skippers were friends of long standing. Skipper Neal commented: "I was delighted to see who had rescued us." He added that when the *Janet Helen* first sprang a leak he did not think it was anything to worry about. But when he found the engine room flooded he decided to abandon ship.

30. Skipper Neal and Skipper Ireland (right) on arrival at Grimsby.

Too Much Water

The mate, Mr Brian Walker, who was 29 at the time, said: "We were only about 10 minutes in the water. It was lucky the *War Duke* was so near." They had first noticed something was wrong when they spotted excess water in the bilges. The full crew of the *Janet Helen* was Skipper Neal, mate Mr Walker, engineer Mr M Medox, deckhand Mr E Wheatcraft and cook Mr R Hodgkiss. They lost all their possessions.

Skipper Neal's wife Ida often listened to the trawler waveband on the radio but that particular day she had not. She told the *Evening Telegraph* at the time: "I did not know anything had happened until our eldest son Michael, who works on the docks, rushed to tell me." Skipper Neal had been making his third trip in the *Janet Helen*.

Mrs June Walker, wife of mate Walker, had been putting the final touches to decorating her living room when she heard of the trouble. It was in November 1958 that the then fishing correspondent for the *Evening Telegraph*,

the late Eric Sheckell, suggested that "baby" trawlers like the *Janet Helen* could solve the problem of the future of North Sea fishing from the port. He pointed out that seiners, which were then growing in number, were not the complete answer, particularly because of the problem with fishing through the winter months.

Built in Berwick

The *Janet Helen* was registered in London and had initially fished from Swansea and Milford Haven before switching her attention to the grounds available from Grimsby. She was built by the Fairmile Construction Company of Cobham at their Berwick-on-Tweed shipyard and delivered at the beginning of 1958. She was 73ft long overall with a moulded beam of 19ft 6in and a moulded depth of 10ft 9in. Her main engine was a Lister Blackstone diesel giving 216 brake horsepower at 600 revolutions a minute through a two-to-one reduction-reverse gear box. The trawl winch was driven by a belt from the main engine. When first in Grimsby she sailed under the command of skipper T Darwood who had great experience of the North Sea grounds.

The trawler was managed in Grimsby by Derwent Trawlers Ltd and was owned by Mr J Northcote of Booth and Croft Ltd, Hull.

The Jeria

"Ship sinking with all crew. Will any who pick up this, probably our last message, send our greetings to our families in Grimsby and to Old England."

That was the last courageous message broadcast by the Grimsby trawler *Jeria* shortly before she was overcome by the heavy seas and hurricane-force winds which had battered her off the west coast of Iceland. Skipper Bill Emsley put out the heroic radio-telephone call around 10 pm on the storm-tossed night of 23 January 1935. The trawler was never heard from again. Skipper Emsley and 12 other crewmen lost their lives.

The trawler, which was only five years old, was presumed to have filled with water and sunk. Earlier reports had told how the funnel was washed away. For a while relatives of the crew and the vessel's owners, the Grimsby and East Coast Steam Fishing Co, clung to vain hopes that the trawler would be found. And the Grimsby trawler *Stoke City* — on her maiden voyage to Iceland at the time — joined in a thorough search of the area with the Icelandic gunboat *Aegir*, but without success. Fears for the *Jeria* were published in the *Evening Telegraph* on 24 January 1935. The newspaper speculated on what had happened to the 352-ton trawler.

"The vital fact about the damage was the loss of the funnel. If the funnel were carried away it might carry away with it part of the engine-room casing.

"That would probably cause damage which could not be repaired in heavy weather with high winds and decks awash.

"Water probably was shipped in this way and, when the boiler fires were put out by the rising flood, there would be no steam for the engines or the pumps.

"The vessel would be helpless except for what gallant seamanship might do in keeping her head to sea. It would be a losing fight and only abatement of the weather could save the waterlogged ship.

"It is to be feared she sank and, as the small boats already had been swept away, the crew would have no hope. How they faced the desperate situation the skipper's simple yet heroic message indicates," wrote a reporter.

Lifebelts Washed Up

The skipper's last message was picked up by another trawler, the *Vamberry*, which only the day before had reported having her mate washed overboard in the shocking conditions. It was around 10 pm, while sheltering in Faxa Bay from a hurricane, that she heard that moving message. Then at 1.42

31, 32, 34. ***below, opposite page and overleaf:*** *Crew members of the Jeria pictured in the Evening Telegraph after the tragedy.*

am on 24 January the Grimsby trawler *Leicester City* radioed: "Heard from British trawler *Blackburn Rovers* that British trawler *Jeria* shipped heavy seas last night. Not been seen since but things were washed ashore including lifebelts marked *Jeria*."

The *Jeria*'s lifebelts were found under high rocks on the Icelandic coast at Latrabjarg by a search party of farmers. First news of the serious damage suffered by the vessel had been published the night before in the *Telegraph*.

"Bridge, funnel, lifeboats etc washed away. Engines out of order. No lights," it said.

Deckhand F. McGuire — Chief Engineer J. Dowis

Skipper Jack Evans was in command of the *Stoke City*. He recalled how he had sailed from Grimsby on either 10 or 12 January 1935. On the night of 21 January the severe southerly gales blew up.

"They blew very hard but they did not last long," said Skipper Evans.

By 11.30 am the next day the *Stoke City* had managed to take shelter in Patreksfjord.

"I went to have a couple of hours' sleep. I had been on the bridge for about 40 hours without a break," he said.

Suddenly he was woken by the radio operator. He told him the *Jeria* was putting out a Mayday.

"She was in Breidha Bay, some 50 miles from where we were. We left shelter and started towards Stalberg but got the full force of the gale.

"The *Stoke City* cost £25,000 to build, which was a lot of money in those days. But we did £10,000 damage trying to get to the *Jeria*.

"The skipper of the *Jeria* sent a last Mayday and seemed to break off. I said to the man at the wheel: 'That is the end of the *Jeria*'. I think the skipper was very brave to go down to his berth when she was filling with water and send that last message," said Skipper Evans. The next day the *Stoke City* and the *Aegir* searched all day without any success.

"We managed to get to her last reported position but she had gone," said Skipper Evans.

Capable Skipper

The *Stoke City*, one of Consolidated Fisheries' football class vessels, lost her own bridge in the storm but managed to effect repairs and make it home.

"The weather was absolutely wicked. It was blowing a southerly hurricane. But we just had to go out and try to get to her. That is the way at sea. No one ever found any sign of her," said Skipper Evans.

33. The Jeria which went down in a storm off Iceland.

Skipper Emsley was known as one of the most capable and careful skippers fishing out of Grimsby. He had a good deal of experience of working Icelandic waters and had been with the owners of the *Jeria* for some time. Before taking command he was master of the *Raetia*. He had been ashore for a short period after the Christmas holiday and the fateful trip was his first on resuming command. He was married with three young children, the youngest being only nine weeks old.

The Golden Deeps

The loss of the Grimsby trawler *Golden Deeps* in November 1932 was one of the greatest tragedies in the history of Grimsby fishing. For the vessel was sheltering from a storm close to a Norwegian harbour when she was driven on to the rocks and sank within a few minutes.

There were 13 men on board who all drowned. The skipper and two other crewmen were ashore and survived. Seven wives were widowed and nine children orphaned by the disaster.

The *Golden Deeps* was one of the best ships then sailing out of Grimsby. She was commanded by Skipper Norman Rogers and had a hand-picked crew. On that particular trip she was carrying three more than her normal complement. Two of them, Mr Valentine Baker and Mr Reginald Beales, were survivors with the skipper. First news of the disaster was given to the *Evening Telegraph* in a message from Oslo which stated: "Thirteen members of the crew of the Grimsby trawler *Golden Deeps* were lost when she sank last night in the small harbour of Breivikbotn in Western Finmarken in the extreme north of Norway.

"Caught in a violent gale the trawler made for harbour and dropped both anchors in order to ride out the storm, which subsided.

"The captain then went ashore with the passengers. In the meantime the gale increased in strength and the anchors broke loose and the vessel was seen to be driving on the rocks.

35, 37, 38. ***below and overleaf:*** *Some of the men lost on the Golden Deeps.*

Clinging

"Fishermen on shore made frantic efforts to launch a boat and go to the assistance of the crew but in vain.

"The ship was crashed on to the shore and almost immediately began to sink. Some of the men could be seen clinging to the mast but they were all soon swallowed up by the breakers.

"Later it was learned that all 13 men on board were lost.

"Some bodies have been washed ashore."

News of the disaster spread quickly on Grimsby Fish Docks and numerous messages and inquiries reached the offices of the owners, the Strand Steam Fishing Company.

The *Evening Telegraph* actually had the distressing job of breaking the news of the disaster to the owners. But shortly afterwards a radio message was received from Skipper Rogers which read: "Ship lost, Skipper Beales and Baker saved. Rest lost." The receipt of that message removed the last slender thread of hope and the Port Missioner, Mr W H Smedley, was asked to visit the relatives of the drowned men.

Merchants

Luis Noreleanker, the Swede who was also drowned, came to Grimsby shortly before the *Golden Deeps* sailed and signed on as a spare hand in order to obtain first hand knowledge of deep sea trawling. The other spare hands, Reginald Beales and Valentine Baker, who were ashore with Skipper Rogers when the trawler crashed on to the rocks, were in business in Grimsby as fish merchants. Skipper Rogers had been in command of the *Golden Deeps* for almost two years and had made a number of successful fishing trips, mainly to the Norwegian coast and Bear Island. Before Skipper Rogers took over the vessel was commanded by Skipper McGregor — better known as Russian George.

The *Golden Deeps* had left Grimsby on 25 October 1932, and after calling at Blyth she sailed the same evening for the Norwegian coast. She had put into the Norwegian harbour out of the bad weather. Built at Selby in 1930 the *Golden Deeps* was one of the most up-to-date trawlers in the port. She was equipped with every modern device for deep sea trawling — wireless direction finder and the latest type of echo sounder. She was also one of the biggest ships sailing out of the port.

Of the 12 Grimsby fishermen who were lost in the disaster, seven — the third hand, E Rogers, deckhands Smith, James and Marshall, trimmer Blake, the cook Royal and the second engineer Stone — were married men, several with families. Mr E Rogers was a brother of the skipper and had sailed with him for about 12 months. He left a wife and two young children.

36. The Golden Deeps.

G. RICHARDSON, Trimmer — W. SMITH, Deckhand

Second Death

It was the second bereavement in the family within a year. At the end of October 1931 Mrs Rogers' brother Alfred was lost near Iceland off the trawler *Oswaldian*. The mate, Mr Otley, was a single man who lived with his mother and stepfather. His father was also drowned at sea. Deckhand Marshall had been married less than two years and left a young wife and a 10-month-old baby. It was a particularly heavy blow to his parents because they had previously lost a son off the trawler *Cameo*. The cook, Mr Royal, had formerly been cook on the trawler *Marz* when the vessel was wrecked in the Pentland Firth in June that year.

Among the first of the relatives to learn of the *Golden Deeps* tragedy was Mr George Grant, father of the chief engineer. Mr Grant senior was employed as ship's husband by the vessel's owners and he was in the office when the tragic message came from Skipper Rogers. His son, who was 28 and lived with his parents, was due to be married. Most of the crew were comparatively young men. The oldest, Mr Berndtson, was 43. Two others, E Rogers and J James, were only 25.

The loss of the *Golden Deeps* was the most serious disaster which had befallen the Grimsby fishing fleet since the *North Cape* was lost with all hands in Icelandic waters almost three years before. She had also been owned by the Strand Steam Fishing Company. The story of the *Golden Deeps* does not end there.

Helpless Watchers on the Shore

The 13 victims of the Grimsby trawler *Golden Deeps* which was wrecked off the Norwegian island of Soro were eventually buried in Tromso. But not until strenuous efforts had been made to bring them back to their home town. Some hours after the disaster, information indicated that the ship had been crippled by her propeller striking a submerged object when trying to fight her way out from the land in the gale. It was suggested that this had left her powerless and so she was crashed helplessly ashore. As the ship started to move towards land the crew managed to get out another anchor. Twice the ship was brought up into the wind in an effort to get searoom. But the force of the wind and tide was too strong and the ship was driven onto the rocky shore. The breakers started to pound her mercilessly, she was holed and started to founder. Soon she was almost submerged with the seas sweeping her. Men were swept from the deck and some who sought refuge in the rigging were eventually swept from their hold. Others who attempted with lifebelts to swim ashore were drowned in the breakers.

On shore the island's inhabitants saw the tragedy but were unable to launch a boat or do anything else to give assistance. Later the bodies started coming ashore on the tide.

Offers of Money

At the time it was suggested that some mishap must have occurred on board the vessel which had stopped her making headway against the wind and tide. Another account said that as the vessel was heading for sea her stern was flung high by the breakers and thrown on the rocks. Immediately afterwards the *Golden Deeps* was sucked into the surf and foundered before the horrified gaze of the watchers on shore. That suggested that the ship's propeller fouled some submerged rock and was damaged.

Skipper Rogers remained in the harbour of Breivikbotn until the legal formalities had been completed. As soon as news of the disaster reached Grimsby there were immediate offers of financial aid from many people in the town. And the Hull Seamen's and General Orphanage said they would be prepared to take any children orphaned by the disaster. Some days later the Vicar of Cleethorpes, the Rev R P Wade, explained how many obstacles had prevented the dead men being brought home for burial.

In his sermon at St Peter's Church Mr Wade said he had intended to add his voice to a demand that the bodies should be brought back from Norway and buried in Grimsby. But the previous evening he had spoken to the vessel's owners, Strand Steam Fishing Company, and had since changed his mind. He told his congregation: "I can tell you with absolute confidence that the moment it was known at home that these bodies had been washed up negotiations started with the Government for bringing them home.

"Difficulty after difficulty arose. The firm was asked to guarantee the price and said: 'whatever it costs, it shall be paid.'

"Then it was known there was no wood on the island to make coffins."

Further problems followed, with the British Consul in Tromso insisting the bodies should be moved in lead coffins.

J. JAMES, Deckhand   G. BERNDTSON, Deckhand

Courageous Women

It was eventually arranged for the men to be buried in Tromso with full naval honours. Everything possible had been done from the start, said the vicar, and the only reason why this was not known was that any action had to be taken quietly. It could not be broadcast because the details would have hurt the feelings of those bereaved. And he commented: "We live in strange times when life was never held more cheaply, when men and women take lives on the slightest provocation.

"But a high example has been set in our midst by these men and by the bravery and fortitude of their womenfolk."

A Norwegian cruiser, the *Frithjof Nansen*, was ordered to go to the scene of the disaster and transport the bodies of the fishermen to the mainland. The beautiful cathedral of Tromso was crowded for the funeral service. Floods of wreaths from the families of the fishermen, autumn flowers placed there by the inhabitants of Tromso, and British and Norwegian flags decorated the inside of the building. The service was very impressive and a large procession accompanied the coffins covered by Norwegian and British flags to the churchyard situated on the heights above the city.

At the same time as that service was taking place a memorial service was being held at St Andrew's, the Fishermen's Church in Freeman Street, Grimsby. Some 20 mourners, chiefly women, were in reserved pews at the front of the church while the rest of the congregation, which numbered around 200, included many fishermen. A number of floral tributes were placed at the foot of the war memorial in the church. The service was conducted by the Vicar, the Rev T Russell Warrilow, assisted by the Rev J Mapson. The vicar explained that he was holding the service in that church because it was the

39. The graves of the crew of the Golden Deeps.

fishermen's church and had stood there representing them and ministering to their spiritual needs for over 60 years.

A Lucky Escape

Tribute to the memory of the crew was also paid at an open air service organised by the Salvation Army which attracted a large atttendance. In the course of his address Major Pennick said it was a man's task to be a fisherman. It took courage to go away with a smile knowing that there might be no homecoming. When he had visited the families he had been impressed and deeply moved by the high courage of the women of Grimsby.

Mr Samuel Turner, of Whitehall Road, Cleethorpes, sailed aboard the *Golden Deeps* only a few trips before the disaster struck. He remembers sailing with the previous skipper of the vessel, "Russian" George McGregor.

"He and I got on extremely well and soon found we had common interests in music and amateur violin playing, his ability in the latter surpassing mine considerably," he said.

The skipper, he recalled, expected 100 per cent efficiency in all departments.

"I believe he was satisfied with my performance because each morning at about 10 o'clock he never failed to put in an appearance in the radio room with a glass of either whisky or rum, making the remark 'Would you like a dram, Sparks?' "

However, Russian George completed only two trips before being replaced and Skipper Rogers took over. He and Mr Turner did not see eye to eye and after only a couple of trips Mr Turner was sacked.

"For that I can thank my lucky stars. Two or three voyages later while the vessel was anchored in the north-west fjords of Norway during stormy weather the *Golden Deeps* dragged its anchor and was wrecked with the loss of everyone on board," said Mr Turner.

The Maw Wyke and the Kyana

Hopes for the safety of the eight men aboard the Grimsby seine net vessels *Maw Wyke* and *Kyana* began to fade on 15 December 1959. On that day all shipping in the North Sea was alerted to look out for the two vessels which had not been heard of for a week. But despite an intensive search the seiners were never found and the crew were eventually given up as lost.

The double tragedy proved that not only the distant water trawlers were in jeopardy on the fishing grounds. Both vessels carried a crew of four.

On 15 November the *Evening Telegraph* headline read: "North Sea Alert For Grimsby Seiners". And it told how concern was growing because the *Kyana* should have landed in Aberdeen that day. The *Kyana* had sailed from Grimsby on 28 November and had last been spoken to on the radio by another Grimsby seiner, the *Ling Bank*. She was then in the same vicinity as the *Maw Wyke*. Reports suggested the *Kyana* had lost her anchor and was drifting. On that day concern for the *Maw Wyke* was not as serious as that for the *Kyana*. Her agents, H Mudd (Seiners) Ltd, said that at that time of year with the heavy weather being experienced, long trips could be expected for seiners.

The last vessel which appeared to have spoken to the *Maw Wyke* was again the *Ling Bank* which contacted her by radio at the height of a gale. At that time the *Maw Wyke* had also reported she had lost her anchor and that her radio aerial was broken. The *Ling Bank* herself was experiencing difficulty in the gale which, although she had a drogue anchor out, drove her some 150 miles to a point some 50 miles off the Shetlands before she was able to set a course for Grimsby.

When Skipper Jens Rasmussen, who lived in Littlefield Lane, Grimsby, sailed in the *Maw Wyke* on 23 November he told the agents that he did not think he would land in Grimsby again before Christmas. However, the *Maw*

Wyke had been expected to land at Aberdeen some days earlier but had not arrived. Another seiner, the *Walney*, had also spoken to the *Maw Wyke* about a week before. At that time the vessel was 200 miles from Aberdeen. On 15 November 1959 the theory was that the vessel's engine had broken down and that she was drifting somewhere in the North Sea. Following broadcasts on the shipping wavebands asking for information about the *Maw Wyke* the Danish fishing vessel *Bodilvie* reported she had picked up a rubber dinghy. This, however, was one of the 10-man type and the serial number was not that of the dinghy carried by the seiner. Broadcasts continued and coastguards as far north as the Shetlands were alerted.

The crew of the *Maw Wyke* was: Skipper Rasmussen; mate Mr L Stabell, of Fuller Street, Cleethorpes; Mr G B McVey, also of Fuller Street; and Mr C Taudahl, a Dane who lodged in Grimsby Road, Cleethorpes.

The *Kyana* was skippered by Mr Trevor Dawson, who lived in Hawkins Grove, Grimsby. The rest of the crew was: fishing instructor Orla Olesen, of Lynton Rise, Cleethorpes; Mr Chris Jacobsen, of Welholme Road, Grimsby; and Mr D J Cant, of Stanley Street, Grimsby.

Air Search

On 16 December two RAF Shackletons from Ballykelly, Northern Ireland, joined the search for the two missing vessels. Both aircraft were from 210 Squadron Coastal Command. Meanwhile every hour British coastal radio stations broadcast appeals to all North Sea shipping to keep a look out for the boats. But the following day there was still no trace of the vessels. However, not all hope was given up. It was pointed out that the *Maw Wyke* had been at sea for 25 days and the *Kyana* for 20 but that longer trips had been made

40. The Kyana.

under more adverse weather conditions.

Agents also pointed out that sufficient provisions were carried for an abnormally long trip. The search went on without success. And on 21 December 1959 the *Evening Telegraph* ran the headline: "Hope Abandoned For Eight in Missing Grimsby Boats". The Port Missioner, who at that time was Mr I D Sankey, had the distressing job of visiting the families of the crews to tell them their menfolk must be presumed lost.

Deepest Regret

The Mayor of Grimsby, Ald F G Gardner, expressed sympathy with the relatives of the two crews. He told the *Evening Telegraph*: "It is with heartfelt sorrow that I learned of the loss. It is particularly tragic at this festive time of the year.

"Thus when I express my deepest regret I know I convey the sentiments of the townfolk of Grimsby and I hope it will be of some comfort to the relatives in their tragic loss."

On Christmas Eve the superintendent of the Queen Mary Hostel in Grimsby, Mr A Evans, and the welfare adviser, Mr W Cook, left the hostel with Christmas presents for the seven children of the men lost in the double disaster. Two local taxi drivers, Mr Acklam and Mr R Scotson, lent their cars for the presents, donated by local traders, to be delivered to the children, whose ages ranged from four to 14.

A few days later a memorial service for the lost men was held at the Bethel Mission, Cleethorpes, conducted by Mr Sankey.

There appeared to be confirmation of the loss when it was reported on 28 December 1959 that a lifebuoy from the *Kyana* had been washed up at

41. The seiner Maw Wyke.

Gulber Wick in the Shetland Islands.

The loss of the *Maw Wyke* was a double tragedy for a Cleethorpes woman, for she lost both her husband, Mr Louis Stabell, and her son, Mr Brian McVey. Mrs Agnes Pederson recalled: "Louis had not wanted Brian, who was his stepson, to go on the trip. He was a lovely lad. He had been to sea before he joined the Army and went to Malaya."

Silence Fell

He had just returned from the overseas posting. Mrs Pederson remembered how she realised something was wrong. She had gone shopping with her daughter and called in a couple of Grimsby pubs.

"Everything went quiet. It was weird. It was the same in both pubs. I realised something was going on." she said. When she went to the agents' office she heard the news that the vessel was missing. Ironically the *Maw Wyke* was only a few weeks old when she disappeared. She arrived in Grimsby from Whitby in late September 1959. Built by the Whitby Shipbuilding and Engineering Company, she was owned by North Eastern Seiners Ltd and managed by H Mudd (Seiners) Ltd.

She was 57 feet long and weighed in at just under 36 gross tons. She had a speed of around eight knots.

The Sheldon

As the East Coast reeled from the devastating effects of floods early in 1953, fears grew for the safety of a 41-year-old trawler, the *Sheldon*. Those fears were to be confirmed and the vessel and her 14-man crew was eventually given up as lost. It was assumed she had been swamped by the huge seas blown up by gales. It was one of the greatest tragedies in Grimsby's history. And it was particularly tragic in that the skipper, Mr Tom Beesley, had his 24-year-old son Roland aboard the ship as mate. Two other men had just joined the ship — travelling out to her to replace two who were sick.

The first hint that something was wrong was carried in the *Evening Telegraph* on 11 February 1953. The headline read "Anxiety over Silent Grimsby Ship". And it was revealed that there had been no news of the vessel for 12 days. A national and international appeal for news was broadcast by the BBC. The vessel was said to have enough coal left for only five days' steaming.

The *Sheldon* had sailed from Grimsby on 26 January and left Kirkwall in the Orkneys on 30 January — the night before fierce gales battered the east coast. She headed for the Faroe fishing grounds.

42. Skipper Beesley.

Area Search

A spokesman for owners Sir Thomas Robinson and Son (Grimsby) Ltd told a *Telegraph* reporter: "Probably we should not have heard anything from her until the end of this week, but other ships at sea have been asking where she is.

"We understood one ship spoke to her and we have now instituted inquiries in every fishing port in the British Isles.

"*Sheldon* may have her wireless out of action and may be somewhere off the west coast of Scotland."

The Fisheries Ministry put out a general appeal for news of the trawler to all ships at sea, and the fisheries protection vessel *Coquette* began to make a search of the area it was suspected the vessel may be. The Admiralty Flag Officer for Scotland was told of the anxiety felt in Grimsby for the trawler, and aircraft searched the sea around the Orkneys. There was a south-easterly gale with heavy seas and snow in the search area. Cromarty Firth was crowded with some 31 trawlers and numerous smaller fishing vessels, all driven to seek shelter. Coastguards in the area were on a bad weather watch.

*43. **above:** The stained glass window in the Grimsby Fishermen's Chapel commemorating the crew of the Sheldon.*

*44. **below:** Skipper Beesley's son.*

Of the crew 10 were married men. Skipper Beesley (57) lived in Garnett Street, Cleethorpes. He had had command of the *Sheldon* for five years. His son, Roland, lived in Humberstone Road, Grimsby. Other crew members were: chief engineer Mr H V Wass (51), of Frankland Place, Cleethorpes; second engineer Mr B Cullen (43), Wades Avenue, Grimsby; third hand Mr H Hess (38), Grimsby Road, Cleethorpes.

Deckhands: Mr S B Blastland (30), Pelham Street, Grimsby; Mr J W Swinscoe (29), Torrington Walk, Grimsby; Mr C A Robinson (25), Park Street, Grimsby; Mr G H Young (54), Fraser Street, Grimsby.

Deck trimmers: Mr T Bell (42), Fuller Street, Cleethorpes; Mr T S Carlton, Bedford Street, Grimsby.

Firemen: Mr K Burrett (36), Eleanor Street, Grimsby; Mr J Haywood (28), Elliston Street, Cleethorpes.

Cook: Mr S King (30), Edward Street, Grimsby.

Only Mr Wass, Mr Robinson, Mr Carlton and Mr Haywood were unmarried. The *Sheldon* had put into Kirkwall to land two of the crew who had been taken ill. They were cook Mr K Hotson, of Springfield Road, Leicester, and deckhand Mr A Algar, of Lovett Street, Cleethorpes. They were replaced by Mr Stan King and Mr G H Young. Both went by train to Glasgow and were then flown to Kirkwall. Mr Hotson and Mr Algar returned to Grimsby. Sometime afterwards Mr Algar went to sea on the *Tunisian*, another of Sir Thomas Robinson's trawlers. That vessel was also watching out for the *Sheldon*.

The owners said that 23 of their ships had been at sea during the gales. All but the *Sheldon* had managed to get back to Grimsby, although about 10 of them had been damaged. On 13 February 1953 the *Evening Telegraph* reported that the all-out search had produced no new clues as to the *Sheldon*'s whereabouts. But it was reported that the Grimsby trawler *Burfell* had spoken to the *Sheldon* at 1 pm on 30 January. Since then nothing more had been heard. And the owners scotched a rumour which was spreading around the port that the trawler was actually in port at Lerwick with her bridge damaged but otherwise safe. Checks had been made with the Scottish Trawlers' Association, which made it clear that was not the case. The search continued and the concern grew.

On 14 February the *Evening Telegraph* reported that mounting anxiety. Several flights form Scottish Command had been made over areas north of the Orkneys. The aircraft went down for a close look at any trawlers they saw, but there was no sign of the *Sheldon*. The problem facing the owners was that they did not know where to search. On that day it was estimated the trawler would have enough coal left for two days' steaming.

Still Hoping

On 16 February it was concluded that if the *Sheldon* was still afloat, she would be drifting helplessly. Her coal supply — if she had been steaming normally for the 22 days she had been at sea — would have been exhausted that day. But her owners declared they were not yet abandoning hope.

A spokesman explained: "We have not yet abandoned hope, for if she has broken down she will have all the coal she wants." A Fisheries Ministry representative told the *Evening Telegraph*: "There is little point in ships listening for her on the radio now, for if her wireless was still working she would certainly have been heard by now."

The *Telegraph* reminded readers of the story of the *Sargon* — one of the *Sheldon*'s sister ships — which was reported lost off the Norwegian cost in 1923. Seven weeks later she was picked up by a German trawler off the south coast of Iceland. The *Sargon* ran out of coal after leaving the fjords and, with no radio to call for help, drifted helplessly until spotted by the German vessel. Sadly there was to be no similar happy ending to the *Sheldon* story. A meeting was held between the owners and the skippers of the trawlers *Burfell* and *Cunningham*, which had been in the same vicinity as the *Sheldon*. It emerged

that, when the *Burfell* spoke to her on 30 January, the *Sheldon* reported the weather was still good and that she was making at full speed for the fishing grounds at the Faroes.

The *Cunningham* had been steaming about three hours behind the *Sheldon* but heard no more of her. Urgent inquiries had been made of agents in Faroese, Icelandic and other foreign ports, as well as at Scottish and other British ports. No wreckage of the *Sheldon* had been found at that stage and the air and sea search was continuing. But the following day — 18 February — Sir Thomas Robinsons officially abandoned all hope for the safety of the missing trawler. They had come to the conclusion that the gale hit her in the early hours on 31 January and that she probably took an exceptional sea broadside and was sunk. Other trawlers which had been in the area reported just how quickly the violent gales had hit them. It was their reports which led the *Sheldon*'s owners to their sad conclusion. At the outset Mr Frank B Robinson had personally visited the relatives of the crew to put them in the picture.

On the day the hopes of finding the trawler were finally abandoned, Port Missioner Mr Albert Broughton took the sad news to the families. A week later a lifebuoy from the *Sheldon* was picked up in the Shetlands. A message from the Fishery Officer at Lerwick read: "Lifebuoy marked '*Sheldon*, Grimsby' picked up at Hamna Voe, Shetland, by Scott Ward, Beach Cottage, Hamna Voe."

The Riviere

Early on 10 June 1953 the Grimsby trawler *Riviere*, homeward-bound from the fishing grounds, was in collision with a British steamship and sank only four minutes later. There were only three survivors from the 10-man crew and only one body was recovered. The tragedy occurred off Flamborough Head as thick fog blanketed the area. And it came as a bitter blow to the fishing community of Grimsby which had already seen two other trawler disasters earlier that year.

The *Sheldon* had been presumed lost with all 14 hands during gales on 1 February, and the *Leicester City* had been stranded on the Island of Hoy on 22 March with the loss of seven lives. Flags were lowered to half mast as news of the *Riviere* disaster reached port, and the whole town went into mourning. The 226-ton trawler was in collision with the 2,841-ton steamer *Firelight* around 5.20 am. One survivor said the *Riviere* had taken no longer than seven minutes to sink.

45. Men of the Riviere: Skipper J B Dunham . . .

Pleasure steamers from Bridlington, RAF air-sea rescue launches and other merchant shipping all raced to the area in a bid to find survivors. But the only three who escaped were Mr Walter Hand, who lived in Stanley Street, Grimsby, Mr James Gambrill, who lived in Neville Street, Cleethorpes, and Mr Alan Lorraine, of Axel Terrace, Grimsby. Mr Hand and Mr Gambrill were deckhands and Mr Lorraine a fireman. All three are still alive and still living locally.

The one body recovered was that of third hand Mr William Duncan, who was in his early 50s and lived in Welholme Road, Grimsby. Those who died included Skipper Ben Dunham, who was last seen waist-deep in water shouting to his crew: "Go forward, the ship's going down."

Among the aircraft taking part in the desperate search for survivors was a Lincoln from Manby RAF Flying College. A spokesman there told the *Evening Telegraph* at the time that the aircraft had returned after 45 minutes, the pilot reporting dense fog over the area which made searching impossible. The Bridlington pleasure boat *Thornwick* also made for the scene to join in the effort. Two of the vessel's crew, J White and K Lester, told reporters: "We heard a wireless message and left Bridlington harbour to a position seven miles north-east of Flamborough Head, where we went alongside the *Suntrap*, a

46. . . Mate C F Hanniman . . .

collier bound for London, who reported wreckage about a mile astern.

"We went to that position and saw wreckage — fish baskets and small pieces of wood — but there was no trace of any survivor."

The Flamborough lifeboat, which had found its way through the fog to the scene, eventually took the three survivors on board and carried them to safety. She was unable to get close in to the North Landing at Flamborough and consequently the shipwrecked men were carried ashore on the backs of the lifeboat-launching staff who waded deep into the sea to fetch them. As soon as they had been landed the lifeboat returned to take up the search once again.

The vessel also landed a liferaft and lifebelt from the *Riviere*. Shocked and exhausted, the battered survivors were taken to the North Star private hotel at Flamborough, where they were given food and hot drinks and then had hot baths before going to bed.

The *Riviere*, which was built in Beverley in 1916, had left on a fishing trip to the Faroes grounds on 30 May. She had been fishing off the north coast of Scotland on her way back and had been expected in Grimsby later on 10 June — the day she sank. Brief radio messages had given first news of the disaster. Cullercoates Radio reported a message from the *Firelight* giving her position and stating briefly: "In collision with trawler *Riviere* of Grimsby at 5.20 am. Trawler sunk. Our lifeboat launched." Cullercoates later reported: "At 6.25 *Firelight* reported lifeboat returned with three survivors who report original crew of 13 and trawler's lifeboat not launched.

"Am cruising in vicinity of position searching for possible survivors, visibility poor." None was to be found.

When he felt fit to talk fireman Lorraine told reporters at the time how there had been no chance to get the lifeboat out. He had just stoked up when he heard a loud crash and the second engineer went in and said they had been struck.

Sinking Body

Mr Lorraine went on: "I went on deck and the skipper was up to his waist in water. There was no time to get the boat out.

"The skipper told us to go forward on the ship but we could not do so as she was sinking so fast. Then I was in the water.

"I grabbed a deckraft and was holding on to it when a lifeboat lowered from the *Firelight* came and picked us up.

"We were having breakfast on the *Firelight* when the Flamborough lifeboat came and took us on."

Mr Lorraine added that when they were returning to shore in the lifeboat they picked up the body of third hand Duncan. They also saw the body of another crewman, possibly the second engineer, but it sank before they reached it. Mr Lorraine was making his fourth trip with the vessel. He had been a fisherman since he was 15, although during the war he had served as a cook with the Royal Navy.

47. . . Survivors, W Hand (left) and A Lorraine . . .

Gaping Hole

Another of the survivors, deckhand Gambrill, told how he was in his bunk when the violent collision occurred. He went on deck to find that the large steamer had ploughed into the 37-year-old trawler. He told waiting reporters: "I got a lifebelt and was going with two others to launch our lifeboat when the *Firelight* went astern and left a gaping hole.

"The water rushed in and the trawler sank in a few minutes. The rest of the crew went forward and only those who were astern have been saved."

Mr Gambrill, whose late father was a North Sea skipper, had gone back to sea the previous Christmas after serving in the Royal Corps of Signals for six years. He had seen service in Korea for nearly a year. Coincidentally the atrocious foggy conditions caused problems for other shipping in the North Sea the same day.

Tragic End

As the *Riviere* sank beneath him, third hand Mr W Duncan cut away his own clothing in an effort to stay afloat. But despite his courageous efforts he became one of ten men to die in the tragedy. And his was the only body recovered. Mr William Duncan told how he had heard that his father, also William, had been picked up more than five hours after the collision.

"When they found him he had a gutting knife in his hand which he had used to cut his clothes away to help stay afloat. He was a powerful swimmer," said Mr Duncan. Ironically his father had intended to leave the sea at the end of that summer. Married with a married son and daughter, he told his wife he could not stand up to another winter at sea and was coming ashore for good. Aged 54 he had been at sea since he was 16 and had served with the Royal Navy during the First World War. Mr Duncan junior remembered that a few years after the incident the Flamborough lifeboat, which had picked up his father's body, had come on a visit to Grimsby.

"I was able to shake hands with those people who had picked my father up," he said.

Sadly, on its way home the lifeboat got into serious trouble and two of the crew lost their lives.

48. . . . L Southgate and W Duncan.

Inquiry

The three men who survived the *Riviere* disaster, fireman Mr Alan Lorraine and deckhands Mr James Gambrill and Mr Walter Hand, were at the inquiry which followed into the loss of the vessel. Mr Hand gave his version of what had happened on that fateful day.

Mr Hand said the *Riviere* was a vessel of 266 gross tons and about 117 feet long. She was fitted with triple expansion engines of 74hp and carried a crew of 13. He told the inquiry: "The vessel left the port of Grimsby some time at the end of May 1953, and sailed round the north coast of Scotland to the fishing grounds off the west coast. The vessel was fishing about seven or eight days and the skipper (Mr J B Dunham) decided to return to port.

"On the 10 June 1953 the vessel was coming down from the north of Scotland and at about 3 am I went off watch. The weather was a bit hazy.

"The men who relieved my watch were the third hand Duncan and Alan Dawn, the watchkeeper. The third hand would be on the bridge with Dawn and one would take the wheel and the other would be the lookout. They would change about at frequent intervals.

Siren

Mr Hand said the siren was blowing a fog signal when he went off watch, and he believed Mr Duncan would continue to do that. When he went below Mr Hand said the siren was still blowing.

"I went to sleep shortly afterwards and I can only think that if the siren had stopped blowing the absence of sound would probably have woken me up.

"At about 5.20 am I was asleep in my bunk when I was awakened by a bump and one of the lads shouted out: 'We've been hit.'

"I jumped out of my bunk and ran on to the deck and Skipper Dunham was shouting: 'All go aft to the boat.'

"When I got on deck the bow of the colliding vessel was still in our ship's side. It was in the port side.

"The bow of the other vessel had struck just about amidships and had knocked the winch over to the far side.

"I went aft with other members of the crew to try and swing the boat out, but the vessel was sinking. I got on to the top of the boat with some other men and the vessel went down by the stern.

"I should think from feeling the bump of the collision until the vessel went down was about five, six or seven minutes.

"Gambrill was with me on the boat and I was eventually picked up by the small boat from the *Firelight* and later Gambrill was picked up. Later I saw

49. Walter Hand (20), one of the three survivors from the Riviere, with his grandmother, Mrs W Drinkell, at his home in Stanley Street, Grimsby.

Lorraine on the *Firelight*."

Mr Hand said he could not remember whether the *Riviere*'s siren was blowing when he went on deck, but he knew the siren of the *Firelight* was not. The fog was thick but the sea was fairly calm.

"The winch was amidships on the foredeck of the *Riviere*.

Penetrated

"The *Firelight* must have been proceeding at a speed to have penetrated into the middle of our vessel.

"I think the bunkers would be somewhere underneath the winch, and I should think the *Riviere* was fairly strong where she was struck by the *Firelight*. In my view the bump of the collision and the fact that the powerful winch of the *Riviere* was knocked to the starboard side proved that the blow of the collision must have been a very heavy one and that the *Firelight* must have been proceeding at a good speed.

"The bows of the *Firelight* seemed to be about eight or ten feet above our deck and possibly as high as the top of our bridge," Mr Hand told the inquiry. All three survivors were given breakfast aboard the *Firelight*. They were invited to stay on board and sail to Newcastle, but declined and instead transferred to the lifeboat to be taken ashore.

Apprentice

Mr John Dunham, of Hewson Road, Humberston, recalled how his father skipper Ben Dunham, was on his way home in the *Riviere* with one of his best-ever catches when disaster struck.

"I was serving my apprenticeship at Doig's on the Fish Docks and was called in the office about 10 am that morning to be told about it," said Mr Dunham.

Only recently he visited the lifeboat station at Flamborough and found they still had pictures of the rescue. And he actually spoke to one of the lifeboat crew from the time, who now takes parties out in his boat from Flamborough.

Skipper Dunham (49) had commanded the *Riviere* since around 1935, with the exception of wartime service with the RNVR. The mate, Mr C F Hanneman, might not have been aboard the *Riviere* at all if his own ship had not been in for a refit. He was a friend of Skipper Dunham, who asked him if he wanted a trip.

Radio

The wife of the chief engineer, Mr W Conlan, was one of several of the relatives who heard the news of the disaster over the radio. Mrs Conlan told the *Evening Telegraph* at the time: "It was a dreadful shock hearing it like that."

At the home of deckhand Alan Dawn (58) a family celebration was to have been held that day to celebrate the 22nd wedding anniversary of Mr Dawn and his wife Ida.

Deckie/trimmer Mr Leonard Southgate lodged at the home of a retired fisherman in Cleethorpes. He had been going to sea for about 14 years and came from Yarmouth. Fireman H Smith was making his first trip in the *Riviere*. Aged 58, he had been going to sea since he was 17. The cook, Mrs S Dobson (42), was married with eight children ranging from 18 years to six weeks.

Second Engineer Mr R Dolben (35) came from Scarborough. His wife heard the news of the collision on the radio but did not realise he was lost until told by a reporter.

Wreaths

On 21 June Port Missioner Mr Albert Broughton was faced with holding the third memorial service in six months. He had previously held them for the

men lost from the *Sheldon* and the *Leicester City*. Once again the Bethel Mission in Tiverton Street, Cleethorpes, was lined with wreaths and flowers in remembrance of the men from the *Riviere*. A long legal battle followed over compensation for relatives of the lost men.

Mrs Wendy Newman, of Claremont Road, Grimsby, daughter of the mate Mr Hanneman, told how her mother Ethel had eventually been given £1,351. Mrs Newman herself got £94. It was invested in War Bonds for her.

"I actually finished up getting less than that because they had lost their value," she said.

The Epine

Mountainous seas swept over the wrecked Grimsby trawler *Epine* as the skipper clung to the bridge and yelled: "I do not mind what happens to me so long as the boys are all right. Look after the boys."

The trawler with 19 crew, including Skipper Alfred Loftis, ran aground off the west coast of Iceland shortly before midnight on 13 March 1948. Only five of the crew survived.

The skipper was one of those who died. Survivors told how Skipper Loftis had shouted his last message over the fury of the raging blizzard of wind and sleet. Shortly afterwards he was swept to his death as the rocks tore through the engine and boiler rooms of the stranded vessel.

Chief engineer Mr T A Smith, who clung to the rigging and survived, told the *Evening Telegraph* on his return home: "Skipper Loftis was a great man. He was one of the finest skippers anybody could sail with." One man swam ashore and was saved and four others were picked up from the rigging of the vessel.

Line Rigged

One of the latter, mate Mr Fred Thompson, still recalls how a rescue team finally reached the scene of the tragedy and set about trying to rescue the crew. It took two hours before they managed to get a breeches buoy rigged up between the shore and the ship.

"They fired a number of rocket lines before we finally managed to get one secure," said Mr Thompson.

At a subsequent inquiry into the loss of the *Epine* it was revealed that deckhand Harry Yeates had been the man who finally made the line secure. In his statement Mr Yeates told of the grounding and the subsequent rescue: "At 11.50 pm the *Epine* took the strand very violently, jumping once or twice then listing right over to starboard.

The skipper rang the engines to stop and asked me what I had been doing, and I replied that all the instructions had been carried out. I asked if I was to call the crew out and, being instructed to do so, I went to find that they were already out," he said. Mr Yeates told the inquiry he realised straight away that the *Epine* was wrecked and that the only thing to do was to get assistance to rescue the crew. A distress signal was transmitted within a few minutes via another Grimsby trawler, the *Spurs,* which was nearby.

"We fired distress rockets and lit fires on the wheel-house top and forecastle. There were plenty of lifebelts for everyone. The small boat was smashed in the stranding but, in any case, it could not have been used in the heavy swell.

"The snow cleared about half an hour after stranding and we saw Malariff Light on the starboard side abaft the beam. We thought about floating the liferaft ashore but decided to wait until daylight, by which time it was too late," said Mr Yeates.

Low water came around 2 am on Sunday, 14 March 1948.

"We saw a light ashore about 3 am and fired four Schermuly pistol rockets

50, 51, 53. ***below and overleaf:*** *Crew of the Epine . . . 1st Engineer T A Smith . . .*

51. ***above:*** *. . . Mate F F Thompson . . .*

with lines attached but failed to make contact. We now believe the light was being waved by the lighthouse keeper from Malariff, who had walked along the beach.

"Round about 4 am the water began to rise and we had to disperse to try to get out of its reach, some taking the rigging, some the forecastle and some the wheelhouse top," told Mr Yeates.

The rescue party arrived at daybreak about 7 am.

"By that time I was up the rigging and the ship was awash, leaving only the bridge mast and the forecastle head above water. The boat deck aft was untenable, being constantly swept by heavy seas," said Mr Yeates. He said the shore party had fired six rockets: "Two of the first five fell across the ship but could not be reached from where the crew were dispersed. The sixth rocket went on the port side of the boat deck at 10 am. By signs we managed to get the shore people to pull their end eastwards and, in that manner, the line came within reach of the mate who handed it up from man to man to the top man in the rigging and the only one with mittens," said Mr Yeates. By this time many of the crew had died from exposure. One man had managed to get ashore but the only ones alive were six in the rigging and the skipper and cook on the wheelhouse.

"I hauled in the breeches buoy and made it secure, being the first one to go ashore at 12.15 pm," Mr Yeates went on. "Deckhand Horner, chief engineer Smith and mate Thompson followed me. Deckhands Chapman and Maul fell out of the rigging and were drowned. The skipper and cook tried to get from the wheelhouse but failed and were drowned," he added.

52. ***below:*** *The stained glass memorial to the Epine.*

Charity Shows

Mr Yeates, who now lives in Worsley Road, Immingham, still remembers

the artists who turned up to give three-hour shows at the Palace Theatre in Grimsby to raise money for the dependents.One of them was Mrs Elsie Stow, of New Waltham, who still retains a programme from the sell-out concert.

Those who died were: Skipper Alfred Loftis; second engineer W Tulloch; third hand W Birch; deckhands W Syer, G Robertson, R Chapman, F Moorwood, A E Maul; trimmers L Richardson, D S Chapman; firemen H G Broomfield, H Dracup; cook H A Marsh; wireless operator C H Burnett.

Mrs Wilhelmina Chapman (87), of Grafton Street, Grimsby, still vividly recalls how she learned the news of her 17-year-old son's death. "The Port Missioner came to see me, but one of my daughters rushed in before him. She said there was something the matter. She had heard on the street that there was 'bad news at the Chapmans'. "Raymond was always full of tricks. He used to tie my apron strings to the fire guard. And he was always laughing," said Mrs Chapman.

53. . . . *Deckhand H Yeates.*

Survivors

The survivors of the tragedy were cared for in a local farmhouse and eventually taken by sea to the Icelandic capital of Reykjavik. A few days later there were some emotional homecomings in Grimsby.

Deckhand Mark Bradley opened the front door of his Lord Street home and his wife rushed to show him his baby daughter, Joyce, born only a few days before the tragedy. Deckhand Harry Horner took it all in his stride, greeting his mother as he always did after a trip with the words: "Well, mother, here I am."

At the subsequent inquiry into the loss of the *Epine* it was reluctantly concluded that the cause of the stranding was an error of navigation of the vessel for which the skipper alone was responsible. But that did not remove the fact that among many of his colleagues and shipmates Skipper Loftis was highly respected. And his war record, where he was mentioned in dispatches for protecting his crew from attack by enemy aircraft, showed him a courageous man.

A year after the disaster a memorial window to the *Epine* was unveiled at the Bethel Mission in Cleethorpes. It had been paid for with donations from relatives of the crewmen who had lost their lives.

The *Epine* had been built in Beverley in 1929. At the time of her loss she was owned by the Premier Steam Fishing Co Ltd of Grimsby.

FIDDLER'S GREEN

As I roved by the dockside one evening so rare
To view the still waters and take the salt air
I heard an old fisherman singing this song;
"Oh, take me away boys, me time is not long."

Chorus:
Dress me up in me oilskins and jumper,
No more on the docks I'll be seen.
Just tell me old shipmates I'm taking a trip mates,
And I'll see you some day in Fiddler's Green.

Now Fiddler's Green is a place, I've heard tell,
Where fishermen go if they don't go to hell
Where the weather is fair and the dolphins do play
And the cold coast of Greenland is far, far away.

The sky is always clear and there's never a gale
And the fish jump on board with a flip of their tail
You can lie at your leisure, there's no work to do
And the skipper's below, making teas for the crew.

And when you're in dock and the long trip is through
There's pubs and there's clubs and there's lasses there too.
The girls are all pretty and the beer is all free
And there's bottles of rum growing on every tree.

I don't want a harp nor a halo, not me,
Just give me a breeze and a good rolling sea
And I'll play me old squeeze box as we sail along
With the wind in the rigging to sing me this song.

John Conolly

Ships with a Story

The Northern Queen

The *Northern Queen* — GY 124 — underwent an extensive refit in 1971 to enable her to continue to take advantage of the good fishing which was still going on at Iceland. But just four years later, with fishing opportunities disappearing rapidly, the trawler was tied up along Grimsby's famous North Wall. And she had just one more trip to do — to the scrapyard. It was a sad end for a trawler which had won the hearts of many fishermen from the port, as did all the other vessels in her particular class. The Northern trawlers were invariably good fish-catching vessels, beautifully turned out and talked of with pride by all who sailed in them.

Built in 1949 by Cook, Welton and Gemmell of Beverley, she was one of six of the same class. The *Northern Prince* and *Northern Princess* were built at the same yard while the *Northern Isles*, *Northern Sea* and *Northern Chief* were built by Cochranes of Selby. She underwent trials in the Humber on 12 January 1950, under the command of skipper Harry Self, and recorded speeds of 12.7 knots over a measured mile. The vessel later sailed on her maiden voyage to the White Sea fishing grounds. A former director of Northern Trawlers, Mr John Butt, talked of the skipper as the "legendary Harry Self". He explained: "I would say that he was one of the top three fish-catchers sailing after the war."

Big Catch

Looking back through the records Mr Butt noted that on her second trip the trawler landed the marvellous catch of 3,600 kits of fish — 2,400 of that haddock. Mate at the time was Ted Brown, who eventually came ashore in 1956 to be ship's husband for Northern Trawlers Ltd. On one of her other early trips to the Bear Island grounds the *Northern Queen* came back with 2,987 kits — 2000 of which were left unsold.

Mr Butt remembered: "The year 1950 was an absolutely disastrous one for fishing. Fish was de-controlled and the result was disastrous for the market. The bottom had dropped out the previous November. We had a real problem with oversupply. Other records show that early in her career the 677-gross ton trawler sustained sea damage to her bridge while off Bear Island and in a separate incident on 12 August 1950, was in collision with another trawler, the *Andanes*. Neither incident appears to have been serious.

But on 1 October 1952, the vessel was in a bit more desperate trouble. News came through that she had run aground off the port of Tromso, Northern Norway. Tugs were immediately called upon to try to refloat her. The vessel was fully loaded with fish and had been on her way home. With a crew of 20 she was being skippered by S Ebenezersson. She was eventually refloated without any damage and headed for home. Skipper Bob Blyth took command of the trawler from January 1954 until June 1959. The *Northern Queen* hit the headlines again in July that year when a 16-year-old galley boy fell overboard and had to be rescued. Alan Wakefield, who lived in Hope Street, Grimsby, fell overboard 60 miles north west of the Orkneys while the trawler was on her way to the Iceland fishing grounds. The area was notorious for its strong tidal currents and although the wind was light there was a moderate to heavy swell and the visibility was poor with patches of fog. Two lifeboats were thrown overboard and a life raft was dropped. The trawler was steaming at about 12 knots and the skipper, Mr F O Petterson, brought her round at once and began to retrace his tracks. The mate, Ernest Favell, and trimmer Mr Arthur Williams dived overboard, swam to the boy and

54. ***left:*** *Trawlers on Grimsby's North Wall in the 1960s.*

supported him in the water. They then swam with him some 600 feet to the liferaft. The rescue earned Mr Favell and Mr Williams the Royal Humane Society's bronze medal and certificate. These were later presented by the then Mayor of Grimsby, Ald R S Haylett, at a ceremony at the offices of the Grimsby Fishing Vessel Owners' Association.

During a trip in October 1960 records show that the *Northern Queen* spent a couple of days towing another of the company's vessels, the *Northern Pride*. Skipper at the time was Mr Wally Nutten.

First Class

He recalled: "All that class of ships were first class. They were certainly good ships for getting the fish. In my opinion she was a little suspect when steaming." On 20 June 1962, the trawler was arrested off Iceland and charged with fishing illegally. Reports came back that the trawler had been fined £1,600 and her gear and catch, worth about £975, confiscated.

As the story of the *Northern Queen* unwinds one sees that some of the port's top skippers were to command her. Jimmy Gordon, Len Stanley, Johnny Meadows and Bill Ferrands are just some of the names which crop up.

In the early 1970s Grimsby trawlers were still able to bring in good catches from the Icelandic grounds and there was little sign of the dramatic collapse of the deep water industry which was to follow a few years later.

And so in 1971 the decision was taken to refurbish the *Northern Queen*. The work was undertaken by the Humber Graving Dock at Immingham at a cost of £60,000. The work included the fitting of a new funnel and a boat deck. Mr Butt said: "After her refit she was in the best condition of any ship of her size in England."

55. Another trip begins for the Northern Queen. She was another of the big trawlers scrapped after the final Cod War.

vessels of her size. Her last day at sea was under the command of Skipper Bill Ferrands. It was February 1975. Despite Government financial aid British United Trawlers — who had taken over Northern's — laid up nine of its trawlers, the *Northern Queen* being one of them. And the feeling at the time was that the vessels would never fish again. It was a feeling that was to turn into reality. On 24 April that year BUT announced that five of the laid up vessles were to be scrapped — the *Northern Queen* followed soon afterwards.

The Coldstreamer

The *Coldstreamer* ended her days by being scrapped in an area of Grimsby dockland once renowned for the shipbuilding activities which went on there. Along with another Grimsby trawler, the *Royal Lincs*, she sailed just a few hundred yards in August 1976 to come under the breaker's torch on the old Doig's slipway behind the Royal Dock. It was a depressing end for a vessel which once held the world trawling record. The *Coldstreamer* arrived in Grimsby on 25 July 1955, at the end of her maiden voyage from the Bremerhaven shipyard where she was built. With her came the managing director of the German yard, Mr Bertram Rickmers, who was planning to meet Humberside trawler-owners during his visit. At the time he was proud of the guarantees which had brought him to the forefront of European trawler builders: a guaranteed price and a guaranteed operating speed. The *Coldstreamer* was built for the Standard Steam Fishing Company and had

56. The Coldstreamer prepares to leave Grimsby for another trip to the Arctic fishing grounds.

around a 14-knot engine speed. At the time a spokesman for her owners said they were more than satisfied with the speedy workmanship of the German builders. He said: “The ship will be fishing two years earlier than she would have been if we had placed an order with a British builder. And her engines and boilers are more economical. We shall probably save as much as a ton of fuel oil a day, in addition to a lot of lubrication oil.”

The vessel was the first British trawler to have her gallows and fishing gear on the starboard side only. The accommodation was down the port side. The then Mayor of Grimsby, Ald J C B Olsen, expressed the hope that she would mark the start of a new era for Grimsby. A month later, when Skipper Jasper Pidgen brought her back from the White Sea grounds after her maiden fishing trip, she had 3,000 kits aboard. In early 1957 Skipper Pidgen heard that a German skipper had made good voyages to the fishing grounds off Newfoundland. And he persuaded the *Coldstreamer*'s owners to let him try a trip himself, supporting his argument with the fact that bad weather had recently been hitting the Arctic grounds.

He left on 21 January but encountered almost continuous gales and snowstorms. On his return from the 27-day trip Skipper Pidgen and the *Coldstreamer* brought back 1,700 kits of quality fish. Buffeted by heavy gales she had run into pack ice and was 15 hours finding a way out. The *Coldstreamer* was around seven days on the fishing grounds but the severe weather conditions cut fishing activity to four and a half days. The crew had to cut away ice every four hours or so.

The superstructure was often solid with ice in one of the most severe winters on the Newfoundland grounds. While fishing the trawler picked up a message that a vessel from Nova Scotia had been holed by ice and that the crew had taken to a small boat. She prepared to steam around 180 miles to the rescue. However, it came through that the men had been picked up by helicopter. But even the shocking weather conditions could not change

57. The end of a fine trawler. The Coldstreamer is put up for scrap just a few hundred yards from Grimsby's Fish Docks.

Skipper Pidgen's views about the trawler. He said: "She is a magnificent ship. She handled beautifully in the heaviest weather."

Crew Scare

In April 1970 an infection led to a 'man overboard' scare aboard the *Coldstreamer* in the North Sea. Coastal shipping was alerted and the Humber Lifeboat crew put on standby when the trawler reported that she might have lost the radio operator, Mr George Oliver. However, the alert was cancelled when Mr Oliver was found asleep in a warm place in the vessel's engine room. It appeared that he had developed a cold and was trying to sweat it out.

The vessel eventually docked in Grimsby with 1,600 kits from the Norwegian coast. It was just three years later that the trawler became a world-beater. Skippered by Mr Bill Sate, the 700-ton *Coldstreamer* sailed into port on 1 October 1973, and shattered the world trawler earnings record. The vessel, which for some years had been owned by British United Trawlers, turned out more than 2,300 kits of cod to make £44,678. The *Coldstreamer* beat the previous record, held by the Hull trawler *Kingston Onyx*, by over £6,000. The vessel averaged £2,030 a day with her fish making an average of £19 per kit. It was particularly pleasing for Skipper Sate who for some time had been close to making the honours with his fishing activities. Less than three years later a newly formed Grimsby firm, Grimsby Shipbreakers and Marine Supplies, had the job of breaking up the *Coldstreamer* — just a few hundred yards from Grimsby's famous North Wall.

Affection

Mr Charles Board, of Cleethorpes, remembered her with great affection. "She was a super ship and a great favourite of mine," he said. He was a radio officer aboard her in the early Fifties, joining her shortly after she had had a new boiler fitted. And he even kept a painting of her to remind him of those enjoyable days. More that that, hehad a moving record of her. She was included in a lengthy film of old trawlers which Mr Board shot over a period of around 17 years. He started making the film in 1960 and it ran for around 75 minutes. As a result, Mr Board was in demand to show it at various functions around the town.

58. The graceful lines of the Coldstreamer. Built in Germany, she was another of the port's big vessels scrapped in 1976 with the closure of many of the northern fishing grounds.

The King Stephen

It was in February 1916 that the Grimsby trawler *King Stephen* gained controversial fame when she encountered a wrecked German Zeppelin but refused to take off the crew.

As the First World War raged on the incident was to be reported around the world and today remains one of the classic stories of Grimsby's fishing history. Skipper William Martin was never to recover from the shock of the events and died some time later. Some reports said he collapsed after believing he had been poisoned.

First news of the incident was reported by the *Telegraph* on 3 February 1916, when the "late news" column declared: "Zeppelin in North Sea. Seen by Grimsby Trawler. Waterlogged and Sinking." The brief report said the *King Stephen*, which was owned by the Consolidated Steam Fishing and Ice Co Ltd, had sighted Zeppelin L19 in the early hours of the previous day. It was said to be in a "distressed and waterlogged condition".

The report stated that as the number of Germans greatly outnumbered the crew of the trawler, Skipper Martin considered it was inadvisable to attempt to capture them and so continued his voyage.

The next day a *Telegraph* reporter had a lengthy interview with Mr George Denny, the mate of the *King Stephen*, but the paper was ordered by the authorities not to publish the details. However, the Press Association released part of their interview in which Mr Denny said that in his opinion there was no chance whatever of the airship being saved.

Remarkable Reading

The following day the picture was to become much clearer with the *Telegraph* deciding to publish the mate's full account of just what had happened. It made remarkable reading. Mr Denny said that early in the morning of Wednesday, 2 February he had been on duty and had noticed signal lights flashing away in the distance.

Immediately the crew of the *King Stephen* began to haul in their fishing gear and set off to investigate. Mr Denny said: "I was the first to see that it was a great airship that was in trouble. When we got near enough to make it out clearly I saw about eight men on top of the ship and they were waving and shouting to us.

"The light was getting clear by the time we got within hailing distance and we could see that a great part of the ship was under water. "I should think there would be 50ft of the fore part of the envelope above water; in fact the top of it was as high as our masthead and we had to go close up to it to hear what the men were shouting."

He said the *King Stephen* had been manouevred almost alongside the airship. "Then I saw a lot more men come on top through a scuttle hatch. I counted 18 of them and one man, who had brass buttons on his uniform, appeared to be the commander. "They all had lifelines attached to them from the hatchway and they were shouting to us in broken English: 'Save us! Save us! We give you much gold. Take us off.'

One of the men made as though he was going to jump overboard to come to the trawler. But he realised he was very high up and seemed to think better of it. Anyhow he didn't come," said Mr Denny. He and Skipper Martin realised then that they were faced with a serious problem — just what to do.

Sticks Against Guns

Mr Denny's account continued: "We had a confab about affairs. We looked at the position like this. There were about 20 or 25 of them and only nine of us. They would all have revolvers and we had nothing but sticks. So we thought it was not safe to tackle them on board our trawler which their Kaiser called 'an insignificant little ship.'

FRIED COD STEAKS

A little milk
A little seasoned flour

Dip the steaks in the milk, then in the flour, shake off any loose flour. Have a blue smoke rising from the fat. Put the fish in the hot fat and cook until brown. Drain the fish on paper. To keep crisp put in the oven for 2 or 3 minutes.

"What do you think would have happened if we had invited them on board? They could have easily overpowered us and taken our ship into Germany with us as prisoners — that is if they didn't pitch us overboard first.

"So the skipper shouted to them that he could not take them off and then they all started shouting and saying that they would not touch us if we only saved them. They screeched for us to save them but the skipper did right when he said he could not take them."

"What would their Kaiser say to them if he got to know that nine of us chaps had been able to overpower 25 of them and bring them prisoners to Grimsby? Why, he would have taken all their Iron Crosses from them."

Mr Denny said they had thought it better to head for home immediately to report what they had seen and let the proper authorities deal with the situation.

OYSTER SANDWICHES

Pound the oysters in a mortar with lemon juice and pepper to taste, lay between brown or white bread and butter and trim to any pleasing shape

Heavy Drag

"It was really all we could do. And when they saw us begin to move away they shouted and waved again but I could not make out the words except 'Save us'.

"The trimmer, however, told me that he heard them call out 'Gotte Strafe, England,' " said the mate.

Mr Denny confirmed that as the trawler left all the after part and the underneath cars were under water. It looked as though part of the Zeppelin had collapsed. But all the forward part of the ship was fully inflated and judging from the noise that was going on below the scuttle hatch they were trying to do some repairs.

"The sea was as smooth as the dock while we were there and there was no immediate fear of the thing sinking. But you know there has been a strong wind since we left on Wednesday morning and I should not like to say that she would float long in that water.

"With all that gas in the balloons she would keep up for any length of time in a smooth sea, for although the cars and the bottom part of the Zeppelin would be full of water and be a heavy drag it would take little or no assistance to keep her floating. But in a swell things would be different. The whole ship would have to rise and fall with the sea and the heavy weight underneath would prevent her from lifting with each wave.

"It would act like an anchor and the seas would smash up against the framework and wreck it," said Mr Denny. He said there had been no chance of towing her either. Because with all the dead weight in the water she would not bear the strain of a tow rope.

Mr Denny told the *Telegraph*: "These airships are not made to bear the strain of a pull and as soon as the tow rope was fastened to her the framework would pull out straight and the whole thing would collapse. It would be a difficult feat in the finest weather but quite impossible with any sea or swell on."

Effects

Skipper Martin of the never recovered from the traumatic effects of leaving the crew of the German airship stranded in the North Sea The incident, at the height of the First World War, brought rapid public reaction and all of it was support for what Skipper Martin had done. Even the Bishop of London spoke out in his favour. The *Telegraph* was inundated with letters at the time. They all supported the skipper's view that it would have been dangerous to take the Germans from the Zeppelin L19 on board. There had been just nine men aboard the *King Stephen* and the feeling was that the Germans, some of whom were armed, would have had no trouble overpowering the fishermen and sailing their vessel back to Germany.

One reader wrote:

"Why didn't you ram the gasbag? He would have had no scruples about dropping a bomb on you if he had been uppermost. Read what they did to

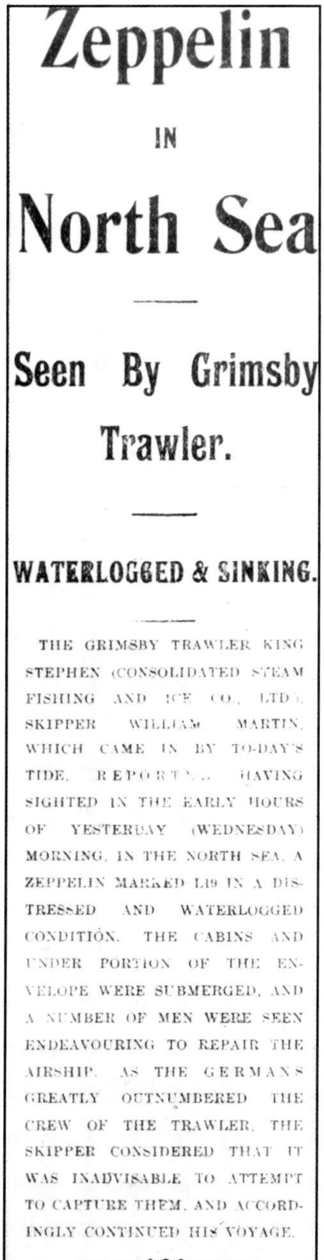
Zeppelin
IN
North Sea
Seen By Grimsby Trawler.

WATERLOGGED & SINKING.

THE GRIMSBY TRAWLER KING STEPHEN (CONSOLIDATED STEAM FISHING AND ICE CO., LTD.), SKIPPER WILLIAM MARTIN, WHICH CAME IN BY TO-DAY'S TIDE, REPORTS HAVING SIGHTED IN THE EARLY HOURS OF YESTERDAY (WEDNESDAY) MORNING, IN THE NORTH SEA, A ZEPPELIN MARKED L19 IN A DISTRESSED AND WATERLOGGED CONDITION. THE CABINS AND UNDER PORTION OF THE ENVELOPE WERE SUBMERGED, AND A NUMBER OF MEN WERE SEEN ENDEAVOURING TO REPAIR THE AIRSHIP. AS THE GERMANS GREATLY OUTNUMBERED THE CREW OF THE TRAWLER, THE SKIPPER CONSIDERED THAT IT WAS INADVISABLE TO ATTEMPT TO CAPTURE THEM, AND ACCORDINGLY CONTINUED HIS VOYAGE.

59. How the Grimsby Daily Telegraph of the day reported the King Stephen incident.

women and children." Another said:

"Let me voice the thanks of crowds today for your great discretion in not venturing to take the crew of the Zeppelin on board. They have no honour and their word would be worth nothing, and you and your men would not be where you are today had you listened to them. Did they listen to the cry of our poor men when they shot the poor fellows in the sea?"

And another straight to the point view: "As an Englishman I feel I must congratulate you for the manner in which you treated those cowardly, miserable wretches in leaving them to their fate which was far too good for them. Had you attempted to rescue them, I and thousands more would say you ought to have been shot."

Plucky

A Yorkshireman wrote:

"If you had to shake every hand that wants to shake yours, your arm would ache and no mistake. Every loyal Briton has a word of praise for you." And one from Shropshire: "I want to thank you with all my heart for your splendid and plucky behaviour with regard to the devils in the L19."

A letter from Wolverhampton stated:

"Well done captain and crew of the *King Stephen*! One of the best deeds done since the war began. You all deserve the VC." A clergyman's wife from Torquay wrote: "Congratulations on your wise action about the Zeppelin L19. The whole people of the country have cause to be thankful to you and all the other brave men who saved us from the hated horrors."

The news of the incident also brought a reaction from Paris. A picture postcard with many signatures had the message: "Hurrah for the wise Zeppelin's finisher." The Germans on the other hand condemned the act as "British inhumanity".

Some time after the event Skipper Martin was to give his own account of what had happened. He told how they had spotted the wrecked airship.

The commander, a young man wearing the Iron Cross and two other decorations addressed Skipper Martin in English.

Reward

Martin was to say: "He was all soft soap." The commander said that if he and his men were taken off by the trawler's boat Mr Martin would be handsomely rewarded and every member of the crew would receive a gift of gold. Skipper Martin, however, told the German he had no intention of lowering the boat because he did not trust the Germans.

"I had all my men safe and sound and I was determined to take no risks. I knew what the Germans had done to my class in the North Sea, and besides, Zeppelin crews dropping bombs on houses and killing women and children didn't appeal to me. Even if the Huns hadn't proved barbarous there would still have been a big risk because there were 18 Germans and only nine of us and you can scarcely imagine their allowing us to take them to Grimsby as prisoners.

"Nothing we could have done would have prevented their taking charge of the trawler, seeing they were two to one." he told reporters. Skipper Martin said the commander had tried all he could to get him to change his mind.

"If half of what he promised had been true I should have been rich for life but there are times when commonsense is worth more than all the gold in the world and this was one of them."

Curses

As the *King Stephen* pulled away the Germans began to curse and yell. Skipper Martin said: "The weather had been steadily growing worse and as no other vessel was in sight I knew the Germans were doomed, but I felt I had done the right thing under the circumstances."

The official magazine of the National Union of Seamen, the *Seaman*, said the incident had prayed on Skipper Martin's mind and about 11 months later he died after collapsing.

It was believed the collapse had been caused by the mistaken belief he had been poisoned. He had apparently received a number of threats from Germans living in England. When he became ill after smoking a cigarette which had been sent to him in a packet in the post he was convinced it had contained poison. Analysis proved his fears unfounded. But a doctor was to say: "He died from sheer fright."

In 1933 Herr Toif Marben published a book in which he gave the German view of the L19 incident. He claimed the Zeppelin had encountered fierce shell fire. Three of her engines went dead and her gas bags were hit and she plunged into the North Sea.

His account said there were 16 men on board. He wrote: "Hungry, helpless and dripping wet they crouched down in the bitter frost." They drifted helplessly until they spotted the *King Stephen*. Herr Marben wrote:

"They tear white strips from the airship's envelope and wave them. Sixteen shipwrecked men are ready to surrender peacefully."

He told how two months after the incident a floating bottle was picked up. It had come he claimed from the L19. On a piece of paper was written: "Our last hour is at hand." A second note read:

"My greetings to my wife and child. An English trawler was here and refused to take us on board. She was the *King Stephen* and she hailed from Grimsby." After the Zeppelin incident the crew of the *King Stephen* was changed. The trawler was sunk later in a German raid on Lowestoft and Yarmouth.

The Full Story

Was Skipper Martin of the Grimsby trawler *King Stephen* justified in refusing to rescue the crew of the Zeppelin L19 in the North Sea?

When the incident occurred in February 1916 only a brief version of the facts was allowed to be published. Public opinion in this country held that Martin acted rightly, and the Bishop of London was among those who supported him. The Germans naturally made much of the event as an instance of "British inhumanity".

Martin has since died, and it is now possible to give the full statement which he made at the time. About an hour before dawn on 1 February George Denny, the mate of the *King Stephen*, saw a light flashing signals of distress about ten miles away.

The trawler steamed towards this point, and soon after daybreak discovered a disabled Zeppelin in the sea, with its huge envelope rising about fifty feet out of the water. The commander, a young man, wearing his Iron Cross and two other decorations, addressed the trawler's skipper in excellent English.

Martin told him bluntly that he had not the slightest intention of lowering a boat, and when asked why replied: "Because I don't trust you".

No Risks Taken

"I had talked it over with Denny as we were drawing near, and after considering all the pros and cons both of us agreed that if we lowered a boat and sent some of the crew to the Zeppelin they would at once be secured and kept as prisoners until we did as the Germans wished, which would probably be that in the end we should have them take charge of the ship if they came on board, or if we refused to fetch them off they would carry our boat and crew down with them.

"Our safety was certain where we were, but our liberty once they boarded us wasn't worth a penny, so I told the commander plainly that nothing he could say would induce me to rescue them.

He made another appeal, but, having made up my mind, it was no use adding to agony or aggravating ourselves, for, after all, it wasn't a nice feeling

KEDGEREE

1 lb cooked fish
1/4 lb rice
3 ozs. butter
2 hard boiled eggs
cayenne
salt and pepper

Boil the rice, pick the fish to pieces, removing the skin and bones. Melt the butter in a saucepan and add the fish to it, stir in the rice, chopped white of egg, pepper and salt. Make thoroughly hot. Form into a pyramid, on a hot dish, rub the yolks of eggs through a sieve on the top. Chop parsley finely and strew round.

to leave 18 men to drown, even if they were your enemies, and richly deserving their fate. I rang the telegraph "Slow ahead" and we began to sheer off.

Howls of Rage

"Directly the commander saw what we were doing and that there was no chance of being rescued, he set up a howl, and the others set up a howl. Their rage was awful. Shaking their fists in despair, they kept shouting 'Gott strafe England!' and they shouted this again and again as long as we were within hearing."

The Everton

The *Everton*, scrapped in 1976, almost didn't make it to the breaker's yard. So distressed was one of her ex-skippers, Don Lister, that he nearly took the vessel and hid her away from the burning torches.

"I walked around her the day before she went. I had a tear in my eye as I did. Things kept going through my mind. I was even thinking about taking her and hiding her away in a loch in Scotland. But I thought people would only think I had done if for the publicity," confessed Mr Lister.

Three years earlier the *Everton* had herself been the subject of a blaze of publicity when she sailed into Grimsby damaged by shots fired from an Icelandic gunboat. That incident brought the *Everton* international as well as local attention.

Her career started back on 20 February 1958, when she was launched at the Selby yard of Cochrane and Sons Ltd. A number of schoolchildren were late turning into class that day because they waited for the launching, which was delayed until 9 am. The naming ceremony was performed by Mrs T B Northcote, wife of one of the directors of the vessel's owners, Consolidated Fisheries.

Extra Bunks

The single-screw steam trawler was 184ft 6in between perpendiculars, with a 33ft beam. The machinery, together with the oil burning boiler and the usual auxiliaries, were built by Amos and Smith Ltd of Hull.

Built to carry a crew of 20, the *Everton* was nevertheless fitted with additional bunks forward to enable her to take 40 hands. She became one of the first trawlers out of Grimsby to use self-inflating dinghies packed in plastic covers instead of wooden boxes. The plastic was proof against rot and weather. Her first skipper was Mr William Balls Jnr, who had also taken the *Arsenal* when she was new. But in the Sixties the command was offered to Mr Don Lister, who was then skipper of the *Grimsby Town*.

"I was quite happy with the *Town* but thought I would give the *Everton* a try. I stayed with her for six years until I came ashore," he recalled.

During that time he came to love the vessel, which he unashamedly described as "my little baby."

"She was by far and away the best ship I ever took. She did everything I asked of her. You couldn't ask for more. It was funny because you felt confident with her. She was supposed to be the sister ship of the *Arsenal*, but they were completely different.

"The *Everton* really was a fabulous fishing ship. If you were on the grounds with any other ships, there was no chance of getting beaten. I really loved her. I used to treat her like a woman," declared Mr Lister.

Mast Broken

He remembered a couple of incidents which served to illustrate the vessel's seaworthiness and her fishing ability. "We were steaming through a storm when she was hit by one sea. We lost everything off the decks and the after mast was broken in two. We lost the liferafts and the lifeboat. We thought it was curtains, but we managed to get her back to Grimsby. That happened on the Viking Bank as we were coming home from the White Sea."

The second incident was off Iceland. "They told us we could not get round the Cape because there was so much ice. But we got round and it was thick fog. All of a sudden there was a helluva bang. We had hit an iceberg." The chief engineer, Arthur Spencer, went down to inspect the damage and reported that the vessel was "leaking like a sieve. It would have taken us 24 hours steaming to get to the slips at Reykjavik. I asked Arthur if he could keep the water down. He got a pile of wedges and knocked them into the places."

Champagne

The *Everton* continued fishing and finished up with some 2,400 kits of fish aboard her. "When we arrived back in Grimsby the berthing master said there was water pouring out of her bow. She had to go to the Graving Dock in Grimsby and have 11 new plates fitted," Mr Lister said wryly.

But the *Everton* was not only known for her ability to cope with stormy

60. The 884-ton Everton pictured with crew and their families on board when she first arrived in Grimsby in 1958. She was finally scrapped in 1976 when the fishing grounds she was built for were finally closed to British trawlermen.

seas. She was a record-breaker, a trawler which could earn good money trip after trip. Mr Lister remembered the days when good trips in the company's fleet of football trawlers brought the reward of a bottle of champagne and a company tie.

"I had made four consecutive trips in the *Everton* which had grossed over £10,000. Sir John Marsden told me that if I could make it five in a row there would be a magnum of champagne when we got back. And we just made it."

It was also the *Everton* which raised the company record from around £13,000 to £17,800.

Arrested

Mr Lister was eventually to come ashore, but in 1971 he had one more trip to sea and, of course, he took the *Everton* again. It was a fairy-tale situation, with the vessel becoming Britain's top earning steam trawler with a grossing of £28,500 for 2,714 kits. But for a drop prices on the auction market she would have made considerably more. A few months later, in May 1972, the Icelandic gunboat *Odinn* arrested the *Everton* for allegedly fishing within the 12-mile limit. After a hearing before a court in the east coast port of Seydisfjord, skipper Barry Green was fined £3,100.

In April 1973 the vessel was in trouble of a different kind. She developed boiler trouble off Iceland and had to be taken in tow by another Grimsby vessel, the *Real Madrid*. After effecting repairs the *Everton* was able to get underway under her own steam.

But her real claim to fame came a month later when, under the command of Skipper George Mussell, she was fired on by the Icelandic gunboat *Aegir*. Britain and Iceland were locked in a Cod War at the time, and trawlers were fishing in areas patrolled by Royal Navy frigates.

However, the *Everton* sailed away from the protected zone, only to be confronted by the *Aegir* while searching for better fishing results. Mr Mussell was later to claim that he had received orders from the support ship *Othello* to proceed to the North Cape.

Souvenirs

The *Aegir* fired eight shots into the trawler and holes were punctured in her port side. There were real fears among families back in Grimsby about the safety of the men, and when the *Everton* returned to Grimsby she was greeted by a crowded quayside.

Damage could be clearly seen in the vessel's side, where a number of holes had been plugged in repairs which had taken place off Iceland. One deckhand brought back souvenirs from the incident in the form of two 'shells'. They turned out to be a mixture of nuts and bolts and pieces of metal mangled together. Despite the events off Iceland the *Everton* still brought back 1,348 kits and grossed £20,000. Two years later, in February 1975, came the sad news that the *Everton*'s eventful "career" was coming to the end. Consols announced that she was eventually sold for around £27,000 to a scrap dealer. "She was in perfect condition even then. She was still a young ship. It was very sad indeed. I was going to take her to the breaker's myself but in the end I just couldn't do it," he added.

Her days were over and the problems facing the distant water industry necessitated her scrapping. Mr Lister pointed out that she used some 13 tons of oil a day, and with oil prices going through the roof that was a substantial cost factor.

COLLARED EELS

1 or 2 eels
2 blades mace
2 cloves
pepper and salt
allspice
bunch of herbs including parsley and 6 leaves of sage
teaspoon of vinegar
water

Skin the eels and bone them if possible, cut into convenient lengths, put them into a stewpan with all the ingredients and stew gently for about 40 minutes. When cold arrange in a dish and pour some liquor over it, adding a little more vinegar.

The Wreck of the Howe

One night on the rocks off Bear Island
A trawler named the Howe ran ashore,
Right on those cursed hidden "blinders",
To remain there a wreck ever more.
No tugs in the world could have saved her
But one went his luck there to try
And found her a wreck that was hopeless,
To leave her laid there, high and dry.

Her skipper was a man named McGregor,
As brave as the brave known to be,
He said: "Now she's a wreck, boys, for ever,
But you'll still take your orders from me.
Your lives all depend on good discipline,
So be cheerful and keep a big heart.
For the sakes of your wives and your families
Each of you must play your part.

But out in that dark arctic region
Just imagine the dire plight of the crew,
with their ship on the rocks off Bear Island
There was nothing on earth they could do.
Their "Sparks" was a brave lad of twenty,
His message for help he had sent.
Thank God it was answered by plenty,
And bravely to her aid they went.

They found her a wreck at the mercy
Of a sea that no pen candescribe.
They couldn't get anywhere near her
Yet times out of number they tried.
On the deck they could see the poor fellows standing,
And who would deny they were brave,
Facing their deaths, calm and steadfast,
On the brink of a soldier's grave.

So round to the lee of the island,
Each vessel sent picked men ashore
To battle across land that was barren
And untrodden by human foot before.
And God only knows what hardships,
They faced on that bleak winter night,
Hands, faces, feet were frost - bitten
But they struggled on without sup or bite.

On the Howe, to that brave seaman, Harper,
A rope round his body they tied,
To swim to a point that meant rescue.
He failed, but I praise him, he tried.
He was pulled back on board by his comrades,
And there on that wreck he lay "beat",
But a hero, if ever there was one,
The whitest of men you could meet.

Still high on those rocks up above them,
With courage, those men struggled on,
Till they found them, and brought off the rescue,
They saved the whole crew, every one.
Those lads were brought back to Grimsby,
And to see them again — it was grand!
We know not one half what they suffered,
But we kid them that we understand.

We thank-you, brave men, for that rescue,
Your deed was truly gallant — well done!
It may not have gone down in history,
It is ever forgotten by some.
But I myself, a fisherman —
Will remember to my dying day,
And no gold in the world could repay you,
Had they called it a job for pay.

And a word for you that were rescued,
For some of you are well known to me.
No words could I write that could praise you enough,
For your conduct, so gallant at sea.
You held up that fine British tradition,
You sent up its prestige, sky high,
Those grim nights on the rocks at Bear Island,
Where in silence you were prepared to die.

Well, that is the life of the fisher
As told in this tale of the sea,
Lives are so often the price
Of that fish you have eaten for tea.
But seldom you'll hear those men grumble,
It's come day, or go day with them.
Just trusting to God in his mercy,
And thank him for that —Amen!

ALBERT HUTCHINSON

The part played by Ernest Drinkall, skipper of the Grimsby trawler Elf King, following the wreck of the Howe on Bear Island, 19 November, 1931, in which no less than 30 other trawlers battled for three days in a desperate effort to save the stricken crew, is proclaimed by all fishermen as the bravest deed ever consummated in the Northern Seas.
Ernest Drinkall, not then thirty years old, was making his first ever trip as skipper. His radio reply to the Howe's Mayday was; "Elf King to Howe . . . Cheerio, George, we're coming along right now . . . 30 miles E.S.E your position . . . had just started for home . . . We'll take you with us . . . Keep smiling!"

Trawlers at War

The Isernia

The Grimsby trawler *Isernia* — GY 448 — began her career with a military name and at the defence of her country. She was built in 1942 by Cook, Welton and Gemmell for the Royal Navy and was originally equipped with one four-inch gun and two 20mm guns. A coal burner, she was originally named HMS *Grenadier*, being one of the Military class vessels. She had a displacement of 750 tons and a speed of around 11 knots, and carried a complement of 40. In 1946 she was discharged from military service and came to Grimsby as part of the Butt's fishing fleet. She was converted to oil burning and renamed the *Isernia*.Mr William Martin, sailed on her maiden voyage from the port to the Icelandic fishing grounds. Skipper was Norman Rogers and the mate was Snowy Tomlinson. Mr Martin himself was a fireman and he remembered that Dave Gerard had a similar job. Cook was Tommy Ringwood.

"She was a very good ship," recalled Mr Martin. A fire eventually ended her career but she was in serious trouble much earlier that that as recalled by Mr Ken Jackson, of Stanley Street, Grimsby. "Jacko", as he was known to his shipmates, was cook aboard the *Isernia* when she was hit by shocking weather conditions while on the way home from a trip to the Norway coast fishing grounds. It was on 27 February 1950 that a dramatic radio message from the Grimsby trawler *Saon* asked for tugs to assist the limping and battered *Isernia* to dock. The message was to bring relief to 25 anxious families who had been waiting for news of their menfolk. Mr Jackson said the trawler had caught a good trip but was hit by a big sea off Norway. "It hit the wheelhouse and wireless rooms and gutted them. The next morning I had just turned out at five and she laid right over filling the galley with water. I thought she was turning over. It really frightened me. I was up to my chest in water," he said. Skipper Sid Farmery faced a five-day struggle against the elements to bring the *Isernia* safely back to port. When she did arrive back members of the crew, though tired and shocked by the experience, related their stories. Bosun D Larn told the *Evening Telegraph* at the time how he had been washed out of the wheelhouse by the wave.

Bad Way

He managed to cling on and pulled himself in again. "We were in a bad way and with our transmitter useless could not send out an SOS. We dodged about with our steering gear, unreliable for several days until at last we ran across the trawler *Saon* and flashed a message to her asking her to arrange

61. ***opposite page:*** *A quiet afternoon on the North Wall in the early 60s. This photograph shows almost 40 middle and distant water trawlers berthed awaiting their next trip to the fishing grounds.*

62. ***left:*** *The Isernia returning to Grimsby.*

for tugs to meet us in the river.

"It was touch and go and we were in a bad state, but fortunately none of the crew was injured," he told the *Evening Telegraph* reporter who had gone to meet the ship. When the sea hit the *Isernia* broadside-on and wrecked her superstructure, her wireless operator had to be rescued from the splintered woodwork of his cabin. He had had a miraculous escape and was uninjured.

Another crew member went on record as saying: "Another sea like that and we would have had it." The *Isernia* shipped a good deal of water. The vessel's owners arranged for a message to be broadcast asking other shipping to keep a watch out for the distressed vessel. Port Missioner, Mr Albert Broughton, went around the families of the crew to warn them that a message was to be broadcast. But later a representative of the owners, Mr A Baden Winters, was able to make a second call on the relatives to tell them: "The ship is safe." He told the *Evening Telegraph* the following day: "They were overjoyed and some broke down with relief. The *Isernia* should have docked on Friday night with her cargo of 2,500 kits of fish."

Eventually the tugs *Hillman* and *Lady Cecilia* met the badly damaged trawler off the Burcom Buoy and assisted her to the Fish Dock piers where she moored until the lock gates opened. Mr Jackson remembered:

"During the incident the Port Missioner called at my home and told the wife that it could be bad news that we were overdue. But my wife didn't believe him — and she was right. We landed four days after we should have done."

Just five years after that the *Isernia* was in trouble with the weather again — this time at Iceland. Severe gales caused desperate problems for vessels operating in the area and in fact brought a tragic end for two Hull trawlers.

63. Last lap on another trip for the Isernia.

The *Lorella* and the *Roderigo* began icing up badly. With the weight of the ice on their superstructure both vessels were unable to turn for shelter and continued to sail north. But eventually the problem became so severe that both trawlers overturned and were lost. Throughout the incident one of the skippers, Mr George Coverdale, kept up radio contact with a number of other trawlers in the area and they were to hear him give the last heartbreaking message that the trawler was going over.

The *Isernia* was one of the vessels which picked up the distress calls but she was on the west side of Iceland and not near enough to offer any practical help. The gales smashed several yards of the rails of the Grimsby trawler's forepeak and washed them away. And one of her crewmen, Mr J Stephen, who lived in Hope Street, Grimsby, was washed across the deck and injured. He was transferred to the fisheries protection vessel, HMS *Mariner*, which took him to the Icelandic capital of Reykjavik for treatment.

The *Isernia* was under the command of skipper J Ferrand during that trip. She eventually landed 1,250 kits of fish. Two years later, in October 1957, tragedy struck the *Isernia*'s crew while the vessel was operating off Fugle Bank, Faroes. Two men died and two others were rescued when a heavy net slithered over the side taking the four men with it.

The men who died were the mate, Mr Henry Jones, and deckhand Mr William Duncan. The trawler had left Iceland because of bad weather and was on her last day's fishing when the weight of duff — a spongy type of sea life — and the fish took the net over the side. The four men went with it. Mr Jones and Mr Duncan went overboard because they were trying to pull the mate to safety. They were pulled to safety by the *Isernia*'s skipper Bunny Newton and the other crewmen who had seen what was happening.

At the inquiry which followed the tragedy Grimsby's Mercantile Marine Superintendent Mr F B Goater said the rescued men had been placed in peril trying to save a shipmate. He said once again Grimsby fishermen had lived up to their reputation of courage and bravery.

The Chandos

The story of the Grimsby trawler *Chandos* is also the story of an extraordinary act of heroism during the Second World War. It is the tale of a German aggressor and of the brave spirited Grimsby lad who took him on and won. The 200-ton *Chandos* was making for the North Sea fishing grounds on 31 March 1940. Snow was falling and piled up against the windows of the wheelhouse making visibility difficult. Suddenly a German plane appeared out of the grey skies and swooped down to attack the trawler. The first burst scored a direct hit on the wheelhouse of the vessel and killed Skipper John Farman Upton instantly. The mate, Mr J T Gill who was below, heard the rattle of machine gun fire and hurried on to the deck only to find that the *Chandos* was under attack. He entered the wheelhouse, saw the dead skipper but also caught sight of a moving piece of bravery. Clifford George Rawlins (18), who lived in Chapman Street, Grimsby, was a trimmer aboard the vessel. When the two-engined bomber attacked he, too, was badly wounded. But seeing his skipper fall he forgot his own pain and managed to get the trawler's Lewis gun which he turned on the German plane. Blood was pouring down his trousers and into his seaboots as he kept up the angry attack on the enemy aircraft. The plane continued to circle above but made three more dives on the trawler with guns blazing. But Clifford stayed cool and stayed with the gun.

Third Dive

And as it made its third dive the lad pumped fire into the aircraft's tail. Smoke billowed out to signify a certain hit and the plane turned and ran for home. Then with his task completed Clifford collapsed by the gun. He had been hit in two places by machine gun bullets but had continued to fight to avenge his skipper. Clifford had lost a good deal of blood. A little later when the *Chandos*' trawl was hauled aboard pieces of a German bomber were found in the nets. It was never clearly determined whether this was the plane which Clifford had hit but it could possibly have been.

Mr Ernest Upton,is the son of Skipper Upton, said his father's body was eventually landed in the Faroes and he was buried there. A memorial service was also held at the Bethel Mission in Tiverton Street, Cleethorpes. Clifford Rawlins recovered, although he continued to carry at least one of the German bullets in his body. And his gallantry did not go unrecognised. He was called to Buckingham Palace to be decorated with the British Empire Medal by the King. The King warmly congratulated him on his action. And the Press of the time reported that Clifford had not been nervous. He was quoted as saying: "The King thought of that. He shook hands so hearty that I felt he intended it to mean all a handshake should mean. He was fine."But the honours did not stop there. Shortly afterwards Clifford found himself in the boardroom of the Grimsby Exchange on the Fish Docks being presented with the Lloyds War Medal for bravery at sea. He received the medal from the then Mayor of Grimsby, Cllr Jas Keay. The Mayor said Clifford's deed recalled the action of Jack Cornwell who won a posthumous VC in the First World War.

Very Modest

Such deeds were in the highest traditions of the sea and were calculated to inspire heroism in others, said Cllr Keay. Clifford on the other hand was very modest about his actions. He said: "I have not much to say. We fishermen do not say much about these things. I think we are too shy."Educated at Armstrong Street School, Clifford went to the Isle of Wight as an apprentice riveter and there joined the Territorials. Called up at the outbreak of war he was transferred to the fishing fleets six months later. Although he had little to say to the Press after the incident he told his mother that when he saw the skipper killed he "saw red". Sadly Clifford Rawlins is not alive today. He was tragically lost at sea just a few trips after the *Chandos* incident.

So, what of the vessel herself? She was a Strath class standard trawler built in 1919. In 1920 she was registered with the Ministry as LT806, having been first L0357. In 1921 she took the name *Chandos* and the Grimsby registration GY1290. She fished for Trawlers (Grimsby) and later for Humberstone Trawlers. She was requisitioned by the Admiralty in November

64. The BEM presented to Clifford Rawlins by the King.

1939 as an auxiliary Patrol vessel but released from Admiralty service in January 1940. Mr Harry Hutson, of Little Michael Street, Grimsby, recalled how as a 16-year-old in September 1943 he joined the International Marine Radio Company at their Grimsby depot as a trainee marine radio engineer. "Part of my job was to service the automatic emergency transmitters which were fitted to many Grimsby North Sea fishing trawlers at the time — *Chandos* was one of them," he said. The set, Type TG-A, was a modified version of the 'suitcase' lifeboat transmitter carried by most Allied merchant vessels.

"In the trawler installation it was fitted either on the bridge or in the skipper's cabin as a permanent fitting, using a full length aerial strung between the masts. It was battery operated and all that need be done was to turn one switch to either AAA for aircraft attack, SSS for submarine attack, or RRR for attack by radar. The signal was then transmitted on the international distress frequency until the battery was exhausted, about four to five hours," said Mr Hutson.

CRIMPED COD

1 fresh cod
a little vinegar
parsley and butter sauce
2 handfuls of salt

Take a fresh cod, cut into the bone on both sides with about 2 inches between each slice, then lay it in cold water with a little vinegar in it for about 2 hours. Put it in boiling water with 2 handfuls of salt, and boil gently until done, skimming carefully. Drain and serve immediately with parsley and butter sauce.

Hidden Threat

But even that relatively sophisticated gear could not save the *Chandos* from the hidden threat of a mine. In April 1948 a mine exploded in the gear of the trawler while she was fishing in the North Sea. A mountain of water shot higher than the masts and deluged the decks; the second engineer was blown from his bunk; and two steel plates were wrenched from their sockets in the explosion. Luckily there was no serious damage or injury and the trawler was able to return to port — albeit three days before her trip was due to end. Her trawler gear was completely destroyed.

The *Chandos* had missed the mine by a hair's breadth and the force of the explosion lifted the vessel and shook her from stem to stern. Some members of the 10-man crew believed the mine fouled the gear. The explosion shattered the stove near where they were sitting. When the *Chandos* docked Skipper P Appleyard told representatives of her owners, Lindern Trawler Managers, that he had 60 fathoms of warp out when the mine hit the gear. When the water shot up and deluged the vessel's decks another Grimsby trawler fishing in the vicinity steamed up to her and stood by her until it was reported there was no serious damage or injury.

Just 18 months later the *Chandos* was in trouble again. This time she struggled 107 miles through heavy seas steered only by a makeshift rudder. She had left Grimsby only a few days earlier for the fishing grounds, but after making only three hauls her rudder post cracked, making it impossible to steer the ship. The crew, showing the usual hardiness and inventiveness of their breed, were not beaten.

Under directions from Skipper G N Spencer a jury rudder was rigged over the stern. Pound boards were lashed to the mizzen boom and bollard sheaves were used to weight the emergency gear and to hold it in place. But the problems were not over.Turning for home the *Chandos* encountered high winds and seas.

The wind was broadside to the vessel and tons of water were shipped over the stern and amidships, flooding the cabin and the galley. Trawler cook Mr R T G Hendry was continually engaged baling in the steerage compartment while the crew took turns manipulating the jury rudder. The speed of the *Chandos* rarely exceeded five knots. But after a full day's steaming she reached the mouth of the Humber where she was met by the tug *Rifleman* which escorted her into port.

A year later the 31-year-old trawler was back in deep water — so to speak. The Hull tug *Guardsman* had to race to her assistance 60 miles off the Humber. With boiler trouble, the *Chandos* was experiencing real difficulties. Fortunately the tug was able to reach her, take her in tow and bring her safely home. But the trawler's days were numbered and in 1952 she made her last trip of all — to the breaker's yard.

The Churchill

In May 1957 the oil-fired *Churchill* became the first Grimsby trawler to fly the Blue Ensign. All British ships are entitled to fly the Red Ensign but the right to "blue duster" is confined to vessels which carry at least five men who are members of the Royal Naval Reserve, the Royal Fleet Reserve or who are naval pensioners. One of them must be the master of the ship. Skipper Bill Hardie, who was taking the *Churchill* at that time, was a lieutenant in the RNR and able to convince the powers-that-be that four other members of the crew were also reservists. It was perhaps appropriate that the *Churchill*, with such a proud name, should gain such a proud honour. Built in Aberdeen for the old Grimsby Merchants' Amalgamated Trawling Co Ltd, she was so named as a mark of the esteem in which Sir Winston Churchill was held on Grimsby Fish Docks. The 180ft long vessel was launched in May 1948 but, unfortunately, Sir Winston was unable to be present. A signed photograph of him was on display in the skipper's berth. She made her maiden voyage in August 1948, skippered by Norman Rogers, who became known as the "Non-Stop Malanga Ghost" for his all-go attitudes and his activities on the Malanga fishing grounds of Norway.

The *Churchill* hit the headlines in May 1951 when shots were fired as she made a run for it after being arrested for alleged illegal fishing in Norwegian waters. A guard of Norwegian marines left the vessel to telephone in Tromso harbour. When a Norwegian crew arrived to take over the *Churchill*, they found she had slipped her moorings and was heading for the open sea.

Fired Shots

A naval launch caught up with the *Churchill* within an hour and fired shots into the air before she surrendered. After she was recaptured, an armed guard was put on board. Several days later fines and costs totalling 60,000 kroner (about £3,000 at that time) were imposed by a court in Vardo. Afterwards the *Churchill* headed home with a catch of about 2,400 kits. The incident led Louth Conservative MP Sir Cyril Osborne to ask questions in the Commons about what assistance had been provided for the vessel and her crew. On 2 November 1953 the *Churchhill* completed a 40-hour tow in the teeth of a southerly gale to bring another Grimsby trawler, *Coventry City*, to safety in Scrabster, Caithness. The *Coventry City* had been disabled when a hawser fouled her propellor off the Orkneys. The *Churchill*, homeward bound with 850 kits of fish, went to assist. Rough weather during the 120-mile tow reduced the trawler's speed to four knots. On that trip the *Churchill* was under the command of Skipper Hardie.

Two years later, while being skippered by Johnny Bore, she was in the wars again when three shots were fired over her by an Icelandic gunboat while she was fishing off the south coast of Iceland. After being interrogated by an Icelandic gunboat skipper about alleged illegal fishing, Skipper Bore was allowed to sail the vessel away. A year later, under the same skipper, she was not so lucky. Skipper Bore refused to hand over his papers after an Icelandic gunboat fired a shot across the vessel's bows. He was eventually taken aboard the gunboat the *Thor* and charged with illegal fishing. The British Fisheries Protection vessel *Rattlesnake* went to the *Churchill*'s assistance. Mr Bert Jones, of Wimborn Avenue, Grimsby, was cook on board the *Churchill* at the time. He recalled that the navigation officer from the *Rattlesnake* had been rowed to the trawler to help. "While they were aboard I fed them with loads of fish and chips. They said it was the best meal they had had for days. Mess funds were low and they didn't have much food; in those days there was individual messing and not the general messing as today in the Navy," said Mr Jones.

But, despite all efforts the vessel still incurred penalties of around £5,000, including having her gear confiscated. Again the incident brought questions in

FISH MAYONNAISE

2 eggs
6 tablespoons of salad oil
4 tablespoons of vinegar
salt and pepper
2 - 3 tablespoons of cream
beetroot and watercress

Take a solid piece of fish, hake, ling, or similar kind, and boil or steam it, when cold pour over it the following mayonnaise. Put the yolks of 2 eggs into a basin with a little pepper and salt. Have 6 tablespoons of salad oil and 4 tablespoons of vinegar in separate basins, add them very gradually, (spoonful by spoonful) to the eggs, mixing well with a wooden spoon, when the eggs, vinegar and oil are thoroughly well mixed add 2 or 3 tablespoons of cream, stirring all the time. Pour the mixture over the fish, and garnish with slices of beetroot, hard boiled egg and watercress.

the House. On 21 August 1957 workmen saved the life of an insurance surveyor on the *Churchill* on the North Wall of Grimsby Fish Docks, after he collapsed in a tank in the vessel. Mr Bill Taylor was overcome by fumes and had to be carried clear.

Just a few months later the *Churchill* herself was back in trouble — once again off Iceland. It was Skipper Hardie's turn to be fined £1,600 for alleged illegal fishing. The trawler was bought by Consolidated Fisheries in the Fifties, becoming that company's only trawler at the time not named after a football club.

Dismissed

On 28 February 1959 it was reported that 10 crewmen had been dismissed for refusing to shoot the gear. The crewmen argued that the bad weather made it dangerous to do so.

Mr Jones, who was to eventually become chief engineer and, at 13 years, the longest-serving crew member of the *Churchill*, remembered how on 6 December 1961 the vessel was involved in a collision in the Humber with the *Ross Fighter*. The incident led to the trawler spending two weeks in dry dock. Less than a year later came another blow when the vessel was steaming towards Iceland. Mr Jones said: "The second engineer called me out and told me that the stockhold was on fire. A furnace had gone out unnoticed, causing a build-up of fuel oil and gases. This had spilled out into the bilges and had been ignited when the firemen had tried to relight the furnace. Nothing could be done with ordinary extinguishers. The fire was too great and the flames were burning the paint off the fuel tanks. With full tanks this was a potential bomb."

The fire was eventually extinguished with steamdrenching tubes after

65. The Churchill pictured when she was new in 1948. She was then owned by the Grimsby Merchants Amalgamated Trawlers but was bought by Consols in 1952.

closing off the stokehold and engine-room and shutting off as much air as possible. Emergency lighting had to be rigged up. Skipper Bob Drew was in command. The incident took three hours to get under control.

Nine months later it was trouble with the Icelanders again, although Mr Jones said the *Churchill* had drifted inside the limit while the crew was repairing a trawl. Under skipper Dave Venney the trawler was escorted into Iceland where he was fined

. On what turned out to be her last trip in January 1968, there was trouble of another kind off Iceland. Wires left trailing on the deck because of stormy conditions washed over the side and became entangled in the propeller. The *Churchill* was towed into Isafjord by another Grimsby trawler, the *Port Vale*. However, the divers could not stay down long in the icy waters and eventually the vessel had to be beached stern first to enable engineers to do the job. Mr Jones said:

"That was the end of her fishing days. I signed off the ship to take a job ashore. A Hull engineer took her away but only got as far as Aberdeen, with boiler trouble. Emergency repairs were carried out and the ship was brought back to Grimsby and laid up, eventually to be sold and broken up." Mr A B Farman, sailed as cook on the *Churchill* when two top fish merchants, Mr Len Kemp and Mr Graham Cann, insisted on seeing fishing activities at the White Sea for themselves. "Believe me, they were grand sailors. They never missed a meal and every haul we made they looked on," he said. And Mr Farman remembered the gift they gave him for his troubles — a white £5 note and a tailor-made suit.

Mrs Mavis Lister,, said her father, skipper George Noble, had taken the *Churchill* on a couple of White Sea trips. "I remember clearly my father taking my mother and myself down on the docks and aboard the trawler to look her over the day before they sailed," she said.

One bit of the *Churchill* still lives on and serves a useful purpose in Grimsby. Former skipper and trawler manager for Consols, Mr Don Lister, explained:

"When I sent someone to get the bell from the trawler, it had gone. I let it be known that I would not prosecute if it was returned. It turned up in my office next day. I was then left with the problem of deciding what to do with it and I finally decided it should go to a school at Nunsthorpe." The bell, still highly polished and with the name *Churchill* clearly engraved on it, is one of the proud possessions of Nunsthorpe Middle School.

The Northern Spray

The Grimsby trawler *Northern Spray* ended her days wrecked on rocks on the north-west coast of Iceland in October 1963. It was an ignoble end for a vessel which had seen memorable war service, taking on German U-boats and rescuing dozens of survivors.

The *Northern Spray* — GY190 — was built in Bremerhaven, Germany, in 1936. Like other ships of her class the 188ft trawler originally landed in Fleetwood. Her first trip into the Lancashire port brought 1,600 kits from Bear Island and Spitzbergen — a catch which grossed just £490. She landed her last trip into Fleetwood on Monday, 6 October 1937, and two days later sailed for Grimsby.

Mr N Woods, was a fireman on the vessel on her last fishing trip before being taken over for service by the Navy. He recalled: "We were fishing down at Bear Island. The skipper, I believe, was a Mr Latham and the mate's name was Brunt. Halfway through the trip the skipper received a wire telling him to take the trawler to Fleetwood."

The *Northern Spray* was actually commissioned at Barrow-in-Furness in

1939 under the command of Capt John Lawford. She then went to Milford Haven to be slow escort for convoys of up to 30 merchant ships. Much of the information about the vessel's war service came from the fascinating collection put together by the late Mr Charles Ramsden, who served as a leading seaman aboard her.

Mr Ramsden, kept a marvellous wealth of mementoes. When the Germans invaded Norway the *Northern Spray* was sent there. On passage she was challenged by the veteran battleship *Warspite*, just returning from the Battle of Narvik in which a German force of six destroyers was wiped out. The *Northern Spray* was sent into Narvik, and there was credited with shooting down a German plane carrying troops. A landing party sent ashore to investigate was badly shot up. The survivors were taken prisoner by the Germans and later rescued by Royal Marines landed from the battleship *Resolution*. Some of the seamen were badly wounded. After having had her complement made up by the cruiser HMS *Effingham*, the *Northern Spray* went on to anti-submarine work.

She was credited with sinking a U-boat, and had to limp back to Lerwick badly holed with a collision mat over her side. Later, after evacuating about 100 trawlermen from Norway, the trawler was refitted and went to Londonderry on Atlantic convoy work.

On one occasion the *Northern Spray* was given the task of towing back to Reykjavik a damaged American merchantman, the Carlton. The trawler managed to pull the 5,000-ton vessel safely home, fighting off a German plane which attacked them both. A shell from the *Spray*'s four-inch gun exploded under the German's tail and he stopped his attack. Ironically, the Carlton was saved — only to be torpedoed on the next convoy.

66. The Northern Spray, one of the company's sturdy pre-war German trawlers.

FILLET OF PLAICE

First fillet the plaice. Then take off the dark skin, sprinkle each fillet with salt and lemon juice. Roll them up neatly and fasten with a tiny skewer. Place them in a buttered saucer with a greased paper over, and steam for about 20 minutes.

FISH STOCK – Place the bones and skin in a pan, cover with cold water, add 3 or 4 peppercorns, a little bladed mace, a strip of lemon rind with it. Place on the lid and simmer for half an hour.

SAUCE – Melt half an ounce of butter in a pan with half an ounce of flour, then add quarter pint of stock and quarter pint of milk. Bring to a boil and cook for 3 or 4 minutes.

Remove the string or skewer from the fish, and strain the sauce over it, then garnish with a little lemon and chopped parsley.

Wolfpacks

In May 1943 the *Northern Spray* was involved in a battle by a US-bound convoy against wolfpacks of some 30 U-boats. In one day the trawler packed 145 survivors aboard, the officers and crew giving up their cabins and bunks and sleeping where they could. The trawler was also involved in what must have been one of the last attacks on a U-boat — just one day before the war ended when it depth-charged the German vessel after it attacked a tanker.

Just two years back into fishing, the *Northern Spray* was back saving lives again. This time it was the 20-man crew of the Fleetwood trawler *Red Gauntlet*, which had struck a reef off Spitzbergen. The *Northern Spray*, which was managed by H Markham Cook Ltd, answered the trawler's SOS and picked up the survivors from lifeboats. The *Red Gauntlet* had already sunk.

Stranded

Skippered at that time by Mr M Peterson, the Grimsby vessel eventually landed the rescued crew in Grimsby. Three years later, on 10 December 1950, news filtered through that the 620-ton *Northern Spray* had herself landed in real trouble at Iceland.

Skippered by Mr Sveri Ebernezersson, the vessel was hit by snow and gales. She was stranded, refloated, stranded again and the crew had to be rescued by breeches buoy. They later returned to prepare for salvage operations.

The vessel initially went aground at Skutulsfjord at 3.50 pm. She got herself off at 6.30 pm although her port lifeboat was lost. Just a few hours later, the *Northern Spray* drifted ashore again at Isafjhoerdur in a thick snowfall. The crew had to be taken off. They went back aboard that night to try to refloat the trawler. But the initial attempts, aided by the Grimsby trawler *Derby County* and the Fleetwood vessel *Frobisher*, failed. It was actually Christmas Day before the vessel was back afloat. Seven crewmen who had hoped to be home for Christmas missed out because they arrived in Reykjavik too late to catch the plane.

That time the *Northern Spray* was lucky, and eventually returned to the fishing grounds. But on 23 October 1963 the vessel ran aground off Iceland again — and this time it was the end.

The vessel, skippered by Peter Fenty, was attempting to shelter in Isafjoerdur Fjord, on the west coast of Iceland. As the lashing seas swept the vessel off course and battered her against the rugged coast, the Hull trawler *James Barrie* manoeuvred close and shot a rescue line across her deck.Eight of the crew clambered aboard a lifeboat and were dragged to safety on the *James Barrie*. The remaining 12 were rescued by the Icelandic coastguard vessel *Odinn*.Ironically, the vessel had grounded in almost the same spot as it did 13 years previously. Among the other members of the crew were the mate, Mr W R Smith, chief engineer Mr J B Marriott, second engineer Mr G Wallis, and third hand Mr J McIntosh.

Attempts to refloat the *Northern Spray* failed because of the shocking weather conditions.

Total Loss

On 28 October it was reported that the vessel looked likely to sink. She was lying on her starboard side. Surveyors who boarded the vessel came to the conclusion she was a total loss. A day later Skipper Fenty, back in Grimsby, was paying tribute to the crew of the *Odinn* and the *James Barrie*. He said:

"The Icelanders did everything they possibly could for us. They turned out of their bunks to let my men get some sleep. Then they gave their own clothes to us because we had left the *Northern Spray* with only the things we were wearing."

He was also full of praise for his own crew over the way in which they had carried out his orders. And so, where the might of the German navy had failed the Icelandic rocks had succeeded. The *Northern Spray* was gone.

Cold War

However, that was not the end of the story. Only three years ago, when the formerly secret Government files for 1949 were released, it was revealed that the trawler had been involved in a "cold war" incident with a Soviet warship. It took place off the approaches to the Kola Inlet in the White Sea on 2 September 1949. The Russians had clamped down on British trawlers because the area was being used for naval practice. The *Northern Spray* and the Hull trawler *Kingston Sapphire* were boarded and searched.When a report reached Whitehall, naval intelligence noted that it would be "unwise to provoke the Russians by making trouble."

One man with fond memories of the *Northern Spray* is Mr Thomas Brown, of Brooklands Avenue, Cleethorpes. He sailed with her as chief engineer from 1954 to 1959 and learned just how well she could perform. He had doubted stories about how fast the vessel had gone during the war while chasing a U-boat. But some time later on the way back from the White Sea grounds, the vessel was ordered to try to beat another Grimsby vessel, the *Thomas Tompion*, back to port.

Like a Bomb

"I opened the engines to maximum revs and we started to draw away. Just at this time Skipper Saxby was steering us past the buoy marking The Binks and committing us to go around the lightship. The skipper of the *Thomas Tompion*, Tess Johnson, took across the Binks, which gave him about 20 minutes' advantage and at 12 knots put him about four miles ahead.

"But such was the speed of the *Spray* that coming forward to the Bull Fort we were on his quarter and going like a bomb, when Tess Johnson tried to crowd us towards the Fort," recalled Mr Brown.

If the *Northern Spray* slowed to go round the *Tompion*'s stern, then the crew knew Tess Johnson had won. "But the man at the wheel of our ship was Arthur Bland, the man with the most tickets out of the port. He pointed our bows for the *Tompion*'s midship, and Tess thought discretion the best part of valour.

"He brought his ship on a straight course and we stormed past him. So disgusted was Tess Johnson that, as he put it, "a rusty tin can" had rubbed out a four-mile advantage and he had a main engine overhaul before he put to sea again," said Mr Brown.

In his 40 years at sea, he never came across the same engine room perfection as he had found while running the *Northern Spray*, he added.

Tough Old Town

You're just a northern fishing town, beside a salty river;
A working town, without much time for pride.
The North Sea's been your livelihood, your taker and your giver
And the east wind washes round you like the tide.

Chorus:
And I can feel you reach to greet me, when I am homeward bound
You lift me up when life has laid me down.
My journey's end will always be where seagulls sing rough harmony,
And tall skies tumble to the sea, beside this tough old town.

The gales that drowned a thousand men are times the town remembers —
We dried our tears and put to sea once more
The streets that felt the flames of war have risen from the embers —
This tough old town has seen it all before

Today your trawlers rust away, a sad scrapyard reminder
of fishing grounds forgotten and denied;
But North Sea tides will turn again, you'll feel the wind blow kinder —
Your sons will sail again from Humberside.

Bill Meek & John Conolly

The Cod Wars

The Lancer

The Grimsby trawler *Lancer* was one of the best-loved vessels to ever sail from the port — and closely linked with one of the best-known skippers, Jasper Pidgen. He took her for several years, fishing the inhospitable but lucrative distant water grounds. She was built by Cook, Weston and Gemmell in their Beverley yard in 1949 to the order of the Loyal Steam Fishing Co Ltd of Grimsby. Oil-fired, she had a registered length of 30ft 6in, depth of 16ft, and was approximately 600 gross tons.

Skipper Pidgen took her from new and was in command when she hit the headlines early in 1954. Penalties totalling £4,750 were imposed on her for alleged illegal fishing off the northern Norway coast. Reports reaching Grimsby said the trawler had in fact been arrested on New Year's Eve by a Norwegian patrol boat off Kjoelnes and taken into Vardoe. There Skipper Pidgen was fined 20,000 kroner (£1,000 at the time), and an order was made for the payment of 75,000 kroner in lieu of confiscation of catch and gear. On guarantees being given by the Loyal Steam Fishing Co to cover these amounts, the trawler was released and sailed for Grimsby.

She had left for the White Sea grounds on 14 December with a crew of 20. Only one Grimsby trawler had been fined for illegal fishing in 1953. She was the *British*, on which penalties totalling £3,745 were imposed by an Icelandic court in September that year. Just seven months after the *Lancer* was in trouble there were headlines of a very different kind. The *Evening Telegraph* of 31 July 1954 declared that what was believed to be an all-time record short fishing trip to Iceland was landed at Grimsby. The *Lancer* had left Grimsby on 22 July and arrived back on the night of 30 July — just eight days and seven hours from dock back to dock. The vessel's catch of 1,100 kits realised £4,238 on the market, averaging around £420 a day at sea. The previous couple of months had seen several 10- to 12-day Iceland voyages landed at Grimsby. Several of the older generation of skippers could recall nine-day voyages from both Grimsby and Hull before the Second World War, but none could remember a shorter voyage than the *Lancer*'s.

Skipper Pidgen told an *Evening Telegraph* reporter: "We had all the luck that was going. We had a good run down and dropped right on the fish to the south east of Iceland and had two days, 18 hours of good fishing.

"Then the bad weather set in. If it had stayed fine I would have stayed fishing, but I thought I would bring the catch I already had back to market in first class condition." But it emerged there was another reason, too.

Skipper Pidgen said: "Another reason I had was that I rather liked the idea of landing today — the fifth anniversary of the maiden voyage of the *Lancer*, when the trip made £11,500."

Mr Percy Powley, served on the *Lancer* with Skipper Pidgen.

"We all transferred across from the *Sisapon*," he explained. He remembered two incidents involving the skipper, although he could not recall the dates.

"One night we were fishing inside the Russian limits and a Russian gunboat spotted us. Skipper Pidgen decided to make a run for it, and did so and we managed to get away," said Mr Powley.

On another occasion the skipper decided to bring the *Lancer* back from the grounds through the notorious South Fjords, off the Norwegian coast.

"The insurance companies did not like you coming through there unless you were in some sort of trouble or distress.

"When we got back to port Skipper Pidgen was suspended for two trips.

67. ***left:*** *Waiting for the tide . . . Coal-burners on the North Wall prepare for sea around 1950.*

But he didn't mind because he was going on holiday," recalled Mr Powley.

Mr Frank Barker also became a well-known member of the *Lancer*'s "family". He was chief engineer aboard her for 13 years and came to know her extremely well.

Mr Barker's daughter, Mrs Lilian Storey, said her father had hoped to continue sailing aboard the *Lancer* until he reached his 70th birthday, but when he was 67 he was taken ill in Norway and had to retire. Skipper on that trip was Mr Eddie Hall.

"My father was a very skilful man. I remember a metal winch broke once and he managed to replace it with one made of wood so that the trawler was able to go on fishing.

"He used to do repairs at sea that other engineers would not have attempted," said Mrs Storey. Ironically, the *Lancer* was scrapped shortly after Mr Barker came ashore. One of the other skippers Mr Barker sailed under was Mr Jim Wright, took the *Lancer* after Skipper Pidgen and commanded her for six years. And he remembered one hair-raising incident when the *Lancer* clashed with an Icelandic gunboat. It was on Wednesday, 1 July 1959 that the gunboat accused the *Lancer* of illegal fishing within the 12-mile limit. In fact the Icelanders claimed the trawler had actually gone inside the old three-mile limit. Skipper Wright said the gunboat, the *Marie Julie*, had ordered the trawler to stop.

"We just ignored it. It was then that they took a couple of shots at us. They were live rounds. Luckily they missed us," said Skipper Wright.

Fisheries protection vessel HMS *Trafalgar* was close by, saw what

68. The Lancer arrives back in port after another trip. She was a fine Beverley-built trawler which fished first for the Loyal Steam Fishing Company and then, after the 1966 reorganisation, for Northerns.

happened and intervened. She demanded to put an officer aboard the gunboat, but was refused.

"But HMS *Trafalgar* did warn the gunboat that if it opened fire on an unarmed trawler again she would fire on her," said Skipper Wright.

The *Lancer* was transfered to Northern Trawlers in 1957 but, sadly, ended her days in a scrapyard in 1968.

The Aldershot

The Grimsby trawler *Aldershot* had her stern badly damaged when she was involved in a clash with the Icelandic gunboat *Aegir* in October 1972. The "attack" by the gunboat during the Cod Wars between the UK and Iceland was described later as a suicidal attempt to cut the trawler's warps. News of the incident reached Grimsby on 18 October and the *Evening Telegraph* announced "Trawler Holed by Gunboat." Although the 420-ton *Aldershot* was in no danger, she was left with a three and a half foot hole in her stern. Luckily there were no casualties among the crew. The clash summed up the bitterness which then existed between the British fishing fleet and the Icelandic gunboats. Skipper Eddie Collins was in command of the trawler when the *Aegir*, Iceland's biggest gunboat, made her run at the warps. The result was a collision which badly damaged the stern of the trawler and tore away 15ft of the *Aegir*'s starboard rail, damaging its bridge and ripping up planking on the gunboat's helicopter deck.

15 Minutes

When the battered vessel arrived back in Grimsby on 31 October 1972, Skipper Collins explained what had happened.

The trawler had been fishing about 34 miles from land when the *Aegir* started investigating a group of 30 to 40 trawlers the *Aldershot* was in.

"For some reason he seemed to pick us out and came alongside us to haul our gear as we were fishing inside Iceland's limits.

"I told him we did not recognise the 50-mile limit, and as far as we were concerned we were in international waters and we were going to carry on fishing." The gunboat commander replied that the *Aldershot* had 15 minutes to haul the gear, otherwise it would be cut away.

Experienced trawler skippers had by this time grown used to the tactics of the gunboats. And another Grimsby vessel, the *Ross Revenge*, moved in close to the *Aldershot*'s stern in an attempt to deter the *Aegir*. Skipper Collins recalled: "He started his run-in near the support ship *Othello* and steamed under the stern of the *Revenge*, then between her bows and our stern. He cut our gear all right, but in doing so he hit our stern." He believed the collision had been an accident.

"He was doing about 20 knots at the time and gave us a real clout. It was pretty bad," said Skipper Collins. At the time the *Aldershot*'s crew were on deck to prevent any attempt the gunboat might make to board her. As a result most of them anticipated the collision and were able to avoid being thrown to the deck. Immediately after the collision the *Aldershot* was surrounded by about a dozen other trawlers in case the *Aegir* followed up with a boarding attempt. But the *Aegir* now had problems of her own, and *Aldershot* crewmen reported seeing many surprised faces on the Icelandic vessel when the collision occurred. A check around the *Aldershot* revealed she had the three-foot rip in her stern, through which the water was entering. The damage was above the waterline but the motion of the screw forced water in as the trawler got underway. Mattresses and deck boards were used to plug the gap, although water still steeped in. The first priority was to get emergency repairs undertaken.

Skipper Collins immediately turned the trawler for the nearest port, which happened to be Thorshavn, in the Faroes. For the first part of the journey she was escorted by the Grimsby trawler *Arsenal*. Later a second Grimsby vessel, the *Northern Sun*, took over and accompanied the *Aldershot* into the Faroese port. But there was another shock in store for the "football class" vessel. For as she sailed into Thorshavn she was met by young demonstrators chanting "Britons go home!" The crew tried to tie up at the quay, but were prevented from doing so by the crowds.

Cut Hose

Still the drama wasn't over. The *Aldershot* went alongside the *Northern Sun*, which was taking on fuel, but the demonstrators cut the fuel hose. The oil line was later restored and the *Northern Sun*, skippered by James Gordon, left for Grimsby with over 1,200 kits of fish from the Icelandic grounds. Meanwhile, the *Aldershot* sailed for another Faroese port to get the work carried out. Initially the destination was kept secret, but it was later revealed as Skaale. Skipper Collins told afterwards how the demonstrators were just children aged between 12 and 15. There had hardly been an adult in sight, although a number of men in the background were encouraging the youngsters.

The reception in Skaale was much friendlier. Some 30 hours later the temporary repairs were completed and the *Aldershot* headed back to the fishing grounds with her new metal 'patch'. Unfortunately the break in the trip meant the vessel had missed the best fishing, and she arrived back in Grimsby earlier than anticipated with only a moderate catch. Bad weather on

69. The Aldershot was one of the last of the Consolidated Fisheries' "footballers" and was sold to new owners in Lowestoft in 1978.

the fishing grounds had necessitated the early return. A few days after her rough reception in Thorshavn, the Faroese people apologised to Grimsby. The apology was passed on to the *Aldershot*'s underwriters, the UK Trawlers Mutual Insurance Company.

The company's Grimsby branch manager, Mr Bill Taylor, said their agent had been contacted by several people from all walks of life in the Faroes and they had expressed disgust at the treatment handed out to the *Aldershot*. The actual incident involving the trawler and the *Aegir* was the second serious one within 24 hours involving a British trawler. Another gunboat, the *Odinn*, had fired three shots across the bow of the Fleetwood vessel *Wyre Vanguard*, and then threatened to open up on the ship. It was believed the shots were blanks. When the trawler refused to stop, the *Odinn* captain threatened to fire into her. Darkness fell and the gunboat apparently slipped away.

Both incidents increased the tension on the fishing grounds. But it was not the first time the *Aldershot* had been in trouble with the Icelandic authorities. On 7 November 1964 news reached Grimsby that the trawler had been fined 250,000 kroner (about £2,166) for fishing inside Iceland's 12-mile limit. An Icelandic court at Isafjordur also ordered the vessel's catch and gear to be confiscated. The *Aldershot* had been arrested by an Icelandic coastguard vessel at Latrabjarg Point, in north west Iceland.

Chased

The trawler was being skippered by Mr Leslie Cumby. And he was in charge again when the trawler was chased by the gunboat *Thor* off Iceland's east coast six months later and faced further court proceedings. But gunboat crews showed their other side on New Year's Eve 1974 when the *Albert* — the smallest of the Icelandic fleet — made a mercy dash to pick up a sick member of the *Aldershot*'s crew. The gunboat, which was carrying a doctor, put out to sea in one of the worst storms of the winter to go to the aid of the man. The *Aldershot* was one of nine British trawlers sheltering off Isafjordur. Weather conditions were so bad that the trawler was unable to put into the narrow inlet leading to the port. The fierce gale and a blizzard also prevented the port's pilot cutter putting out to sea. It was then that the *Albert* offered her help. At the time the *Aldershot* was off Arnarnes, a point which could be reached under normal conditions from Isafjordur in 45 minutes. The gunboat took almost four hours to reach the trawler and suffered a severe battering on the way. The sick man was eventually taken to hospital.

Just a couple of weeks later the trawler was damaged by heavy seas off the east coast of Iceland. A large wave smashed the bridge windows and damaged the radio, steering equipment and echo sounders. There were no casualties and the trawler put into Seydisfjord for repairs.

So Close

So, what of the vessel herself? She was the first of a group of five trawlers built for Consolidated Fisheries by Goole Shipbuilding and Engineers Co Ltd. The vessel sailed on her maiden voyage to the Faroes on 25 November 1959. She was 139ft long and was powered by a 1,100hp Mirrlees diesel engine which gave the new ship an average speed in her trials of 12.5 knots. Her first skipper was Mr Dennis Loveday, who still retained fond memories of her. "She was a good ship. I really did like her," he said. He recalled a hair-raising experience aboard her during her trials.

"We were in the Hull roads and coming down on automatic pilot. I could see a big boat coming the opposite way. Suddenly I realised that something had gone wrong and we were peeling away at full speed towards this other ship."I managed to get control and we passed very close indeed. If I had gone full astern I would certainly have hit the other one."

Spilled

There was a more embarrassing incident when the trawler arrived in the

BAKED STUFFED HADDOCK

Choose a fresh haddock weighing about two pounds, wash and scrape it, take off the scales, take out the eyes, cut off the fins, remove any unpleasant parts from the middle, stuff it, sew or skewer up the fish, truss it by putting the tail through the eye holes, fasten with a skewer. Place any stuffing left in the centre, brush over with beaten egg, cover with breadcrumbs. Place two ounces of dripping in the pan, bake in a hot oven allowing quarter of an hour to every pound. Dish up on a hot dish, garnish with a little parsley and cut lemon, and serve with brown sauce.

Stuffing :
3 ozs. of stale bread
1 1/2 ozs suet
1/2 tablespoon of chopped parsley
teaspoonful of dried Thyme
salt, pepper, one egg
a little milk

Method:- Soak the bread in the milk until soft, then beat it up with a fork, add the suet, salt, pepper, thyme, parsley and lastly the beaten egg.

port from the builders. Sir John Marsden, the chief of Consols, was on board and went to see Skipper Loveday in his cabin.

"My little girl Denise would be about eight or nine months at the time. She was in the cabin. I asked Sir John if he would like a drink.

"Denise went and knocked it all over him, but he managed to put us at ease with just a few words," said Skipper Loveday. He had the distinction of holding a port record of having taken two new vessels — the *Aldershot* and the *Notts County* — within the space of seven months.

The trawler herself struggled on against the background of the growing problems within the industry until 1978, when she was one of six of the Consols fleet sold to Colne Fishing of Lowestoft to be converted for oil rig supply work.

The Ashanti

The *Ashanti* actually began her career as a Hull trawler and was to work under three different owners, five different names and for the Government. She was to hit the headlines during the Cod Wars with Iceland when the British Government stepped in to save her from being arrested by the Icelanders for alleged illegal fishing. The matter went as far as Whitehall and the *Ashanti* was eventually given a British naval escort back to safety. She was built at Selby in 1936 for Hudson Brothers of Hull and initially named the *Quantock*. All that company's vessels were named after hills. Her maiden voyage was in April of that year when she went to the Bear Island fishing grounds. Like other distant water vessels she was taken by the Government during the war and became HMS *Greenfly*, serving as an armed escort vessel.

Scrapping Danger

After the war the 136ft 171-ton trawler returned to fishing and was named the *Cape Barfleur*. In 1939 she sailed for Croft Baker's of Grimsby and was renamed yet again. This time she followed the company's policy of calling trawlers after clock-makers and became the *Edward East*.

Mr Dennis Roberts, who came into the picture around that time, recalled: "She continued to sail with that name even after Ross Trawlers took over the small company but she never made a profit and some directors were disposed to sell her for scrap."

Mr Roberts, now a commercial fishing consultant, was then skipper and part-owner of the trawler *Alfridi* and was looking for another vessel.

"Having been tipped off by Don Lster who had sailed on her as mate, I put in an offer for the *Edward East*. It was accepted by Carl Ross and I renamed her the *Ashanti*.

"I was a great admirer of the tribal class destroyers and Mr Ross, who was my partner with the ship, was partial to naval names, too," said Mr Roberts.

It was ironic that Mr Roberts had come to buy the vessel, as he pointed out.

"Back in 1936 I was a humble trimmer on board the *Cambridgeshire*. The fireman who was on watch with me had noticed at dawn the smoke-plume of a vessel on the horizon right astern.

"He remarked it was probably one of the new Yorkies with forced-draught, and would overtake us by dinner.

"Sure enough, as we went off watch, there was the sleek new trawler *Quantock* steaming past us, leaving us behind. How was I to know at that moment that I would become the registered managing owner of her some 22 years later," said Mr Roberts.

Public Eye

As the *Ashanti*, the vessel was to make news several times as the top ship of the week. Being a plaice specialist, Mr Roberts, who skippered her, was not affected by heavy cod landings and the catch often sold very well when other more successful ships with better-known skippers were feeding the fishmeal factory. In the late '50s when Britain and Iceland were locked in a Cod War, the *Ashanti* was once again in the public eye. Mr Roberts related the most famous story of them all.

"I had left the vessel to my mate, Arthur Cook, to skipper for two trips while I served as liaison skipper with the Navy. "Inadvertently, in an area bad for precise navigation, Arthur had gone very close to the four-mile limit and the Icelandic gunboat *Thor* apprehended him. He was saved in the nick of time by the Navy, as HMS *Barbarossa* arrived on the scene.

"This was an international incident as the British Trawlers Federation had decreed that any of their vessels caught within the four-mile limit should not be defended but had to stand trial at Iceland," said Mr Roberts. However, he was not a member of the BTF and, as the registered owner of the *Ashanti* was able to ignore their dictate.

Gunboat Shadow

For the rest of the voyage the Icelandic gunboat *Thor* hugged our vessel with the *Barbarossa* in attendance. Some 10 days later we recalled her and the *Thor* followed her all the way to Faroe Bank to try to get her back.

"When the *Thor* gave up the chase the captain of the *Barbarossa* asked Skipper Cook to visit him, and they discovered to their surprise they had been shipmates during the war," said Mr Roberts.

Skipper Cook,also remembered the incident well.

"I think when it all blew up they had a meeting in Grimsby but that it eventually went as far as Whitehall.

70, 71. ***below and overleaf:*** *The Ashanti pictured shortly before she was sold to Belgian scrap dealers in 1960. She was built in 1936 and first sailed from Hull as the Quantock and later the Cape Barfleur. She was bought by Croft Bakers and came to Grimsby in 1949 and was renamed Edward East and took her fourth and final name just three years before she finished fishing.*

"I actually recognised the voice of the Navy captain. I had known him during the war.

"It was certainly a bit of a funny feeling having the gunboats after us. Every time you looked up there was the gunboat on our trail," said Skipper Cook.

Amusing Incident

He had generally fond memories of the *Ashanti*. "She was a grand old ship. We had only a few crew changes. She was a happy ship." Chief engineer at the time was Mr Norman Crampton.

"She might have been an old ship but her engines gave me no trouble at all. They were in excellent shape," he said. He, too, remembered that famous incident, and did so with a certain amusement. "You had to be there to appreciate it," he said. The *Ashanti* had been on the west side of Iceland when they were approached by the Icelandic gunboats, he explained.

"The *Barbarossa* decided to take us to the east side. They asked us how fast we could go and I said about 11 knots. But we overtook him on the way. He told us we were doing 12 knots then!" said Mr Crampton. As well as the gunboats the Icelandic Catalina aircraft used by the coastguard was also on the scene.

"They were waiting to grab us when they got the opportunity. But the *Barbarossa* stuck with us, and we caught a bloody good trip," said Mr Crampton. The Icelandic gunboat skipper contacted the *Ashanti* and asked if there was any news from England about the vessel giving up. He wanted to take the trawler in.

"We told him we had news and that was that we were heading home. But he refused to give up. The gunboat and the plane followed us all the way to the Faroes, but we had the *Barbarossa* with us," said Mr Crampton.

News Scoop

Mr Roberts remembered Mr Crampton. "He used to tell me what was going to happen before it did. He was a good man to have along. I used to pay him a bit over the odds," he said.

Grimsby freelance journalist Mr Charles Ekberg got a bit of a scoop when

the *Ashanti* came home. Mr Roberts was anxious that the crew avoid the world's Press which was waiting for the vessel in Grimsby. To that end he invited Mr Ekberg to accompany him and went to meet the vessel in Scarborough. Mr Ekberg said: "They had a recording of the incident aboard the trawler. When the gunboat came too close they had turned the deck hose on it. All you heard coming back was: 'British bastards. You have put out the galley fire.' " He remembered, too, that the trawler's theme song at the time was "She's only Ashanti in old shanty town!" Mr Roberts took over the job of skipper again after that confrontation with the Icelanders.

"I went straight back to Iceland where their gunboats were waiting. But we had a good device which was thought up by one of our deckhands, Tommy Matthews, who suggested rigging up the port side trawl on the derricks so that if we were boarded, the Icelanders would be delayed quick access.

"This had become common practice by most of the trawlers and certainly saved a lot of anxiety," said Mr Roberts.

But the *Ashanti* was almost caught out a few weeks later. Mr Roberts said: "Both trawls were stowed away and we were bound homewards with a good trip. There was rather nasty weather and I was close inshore when the small gunboat *Albert* came out of Reykjanes Bay and fired shots.

"He came to within 25 yards, firing point-blank. But they were blank cartridges and we kept our course until out into deeper water where the sea was rough and his gunners could not operate."

The attempts by the Icelanders to get the *Ashanti* continued.

"I had sent Captain Christofferson, head of the Icelandic coastguard, a Christmas card.

"A few months later, when they tried to board again and failed, over the loud-hailer came the message: 'The Captain thanks you for your Christmas greetings and will reply when he gets you into court.' "

"They never did, of course. I had an alert and loyal crew and we all treated it as great fun — for most of the time," recalled Mr Roberts.

Sadly, with the extension of limits the usefulness of old vessels like the *Ashanti* came to an end. Mr Roberts sold his vessels to Ross and stayed ashore as operations director for Ross Trawlers. The *Ashanti* finally went to the breakers' yard in the early '60s.

Harry Eddom

High on the storm torn coast of Iceland,
February, 'Sixty eight,
Ross Cleveland out of Hull lay hiding;
With anxious eyes her skipper waits.

Gale force twelve and the black ice building;
Blinding snow, and the radar gone —
On the cruel rocks of Isafjord
She'll be thrown before dawn.

Try to run for the eastern seaboard —
Turn her head into the gale;
Harry Eddom leaves the wheelhouse —
Steps into that howling hell.

Down to a grave in the icy waters —
Down to a grave in the cruel sea;
Over goes the good Ross Cleveland —
Ten seconds to eternity . . .

Out in a raft on the boiling water —
Bitter wind cuts like a knife.
Two men freeze and die beside him
As Harry Eddom clings to his life.

Morning comes and the raft is grounded;
Three men lie as stone.
Consciousness at last returning
One man walks ashore alone . . .

Cold are the shores of the Isafjord,
Harsh and bare her rocky crest;
All day, all night walks Harry Eddom —
A dead man if he stops to rest.

In the misty light of an Iceland morning,
Over the rocks in the drifting rain,
Shepherds bring poor Harry Eddom
Back from the dead to sail again.

Bill Meek & John Conolly

In February 1968 the trawler Ross Cleveland was overwhelmed by black ice and sank in Isafjord, Iceland.
The radio reported no survivors. Two days later Harry Eddom was found by local shepherds after wandering the shores of the fjord in the worst of weather. Shortly afterwards, he was back at sea again.

Foreign Affairs

The Rona Hansen

It is 21 years since the Grimsby seine net vessel *Rona Hansen* sank in the North Sea and her skipper is now convinced she was struck by a Russian submarine. The vessel went down very quickly after the incident on 3 November 1963. Luckily the three-man crew was able to take to a liferaft before the vessel finally disappeared.

They were later picked up by the Norwegian liner *Leda*. At times there was speculation that the vessel, which had only been launched four years before, had in fact been struck by a submarine. First information suggested it was a Danish vessel but this was later discounted by both the Danish authorities and the rescued crew.

After that came the belief that the 61ft *Rona Hansen* had been in collision with some other submerged object.

Convinced

Her skipper, Mr Henry Hansen, is convinced that object was a Russian submarine.

He said: "The Danish submarine, the *Delfinen*, came to help us. We did not hit her. It was a Russian submarine which had been seen in the area."

Skipper Hansen said a naval exercise was taking place in the area at the time. "The Russian was possibly spying or something," he said.

A fellow skipper told him later than he had seen the unmarked submarine surfaced for some three days in the area where the *Rona Hansen* eventually went down. "He was having repairs to his tower. I am convinced that was what hit us," said Skipper Hansen.

Liability

Of course, he was unable to claim any compensation because no one would admit liability.

The *Rona Hansen* sank about 80 miles from the Norwegian coast. And a Danish naval spokesman said in Copenhagen, the day after the incident, that the Danish submarine *Delfinen* was in the area where the *Rona Hansen* sank but not at the position given by the Grimsby vessel immediately after the collision. The Danish had in fact been ordered to search for the *Rona Hansen*'s crew but he emphasised that no Danish vessel had been involved in the collision.

The three man crew of the *Rona Hansen* was Skipper Henry Hansen, who then lived in Rymer Place, Cleethorpes; mate Peter Cullen, who lived in Pelham Street, Grimsby; and deckie/cook Tony Chester who was just 17 and lived in Sixhills Street, Grimsby. The seiner had left Grimsby on Wednesday 30 October for a North Sea trip. It was on Saturday night that disaster struck.

Dozing

The vessel was steaming towards the fishing grounds at around 8 knots. At about 10 pm Skipper Hansen went to his cabin, leaving the mate Peter Cullen at the wheel. Skipper was later to tell the *Evening Telegraph*: "I was just dozing off at 11.30 pm when I felt the ship bump. It was as if we had stopped. I heard something bumping off the propellor. I began shouting to the mate and told him to look behind to see if we had struck anything. He came back and said we were filling with water and I told him to get the cook out and launch the rubber dinghy."

Skipper Hansen said he knew by that time that something serious had

*72. **left:** Trawlers tied up at Grimsby against a long gone terrace of houses in the great strike of 1901.*

happened because water was pouring all over the ship.

"I took it the bottom had been torn out because water was coming in so quickly." he said.

Distress

Skipper Hansen managed to get a distress call out on the radio. At that stage two signal distress rockets were fired. But as the men fired off a third it rose a mere 10 yards or so into the air, exploded and began spiralling downwards towards the dinghy which was alongside the seiner.

Skipper Hansen told reporters: "It was our most anxious moment. We dare not launch any more for fear of them falling into the dinghy and setting it alight." The rapidly-sent radio messages meanwhile had brought a quick response from the Norwegian liner *Leda*. She radioed back that she would be on the scene in two hours. Hastily the men leapt aboard the dinghy.

First Class

The *Rona Hansen* went down almost immediately afterwards. "She went over backwards and the rigging nearly caught us and pulled us down," recalled Skipper Hansen. For the next two hours the crew paddled around in the dinghy. Then the *Leda* came and took them on board. The crew were well cared for aboard the Norwegian ship and even got a meal in the first class saloon. They were eventually landed in Newcastle and made the remainder of the journey back to Grimsby by car.

The mate, Mr Cullen, told waiting reporters of being on watch shortly before midnight on the fateful night.

"I was in the wheelhouse when all of a sudden I felt a bump and the ship stopped dead. Then it went forward again as though it was sliding over something. I shouted to the skipper: 'Ease the engine down.' I went to look

73. The seiner Rona Hansen with crew and families on board.

over the side but could not see anything. I then heard water in the engine room," he said.

Position

Mr Cullen roused the cook, who was off watch, and by the time he was out of his bunk the skipper had launched the liferaft. Mr Cullen said at the time: "I looked in the fish room and it was just about full of water. We sent rockets up and the skipper was putting out Mayday calls giving our position. We all got in the liferaft and 5 or10 minutes later we saw the *Rona* go down. She came up again and finally went down." It was around 1.10 am on the Sunday. The *Leda* was unable to come up close to the side of the dinghy and so a launch was put out to carry the men to safety. Mr Cullen commented: "Perhaps the funniest incident was when we were sitting with no boots on and in our dirty clothes eating kippers with the first class passengers." Mr Chester salvaged a clock from the sinking vessel. And that enabled him afterwards to record how they were in the liferaft at 12.55 am. It was 1.10 am when the ship sank.

Two Ships

At 2.30 am they spotted two ships steaming to the spot and at 3.30 am they were safely aboard the *Leda*. It was his first trip in the *Rona Hansen*. The trip before that he was on board the trawler *Trueman* when two men died in a raging fire in the engine room.

He told the *Evening Telegraph*: "That time I came back from Norway aboard the *Leda* and when I was picked up form the liferaft this time one of the crew said 'I have seen you before, haven't I?' " The *Rona Hansen* was part owned by Mr Hansen and Mr Klemens Kowal. She was named after Skipper Hansen's daughter Rona. When she was launched by Rona in 1959 she was the first seiner of its type in Grimsby to have a refrigerator fitted in the galley to store the crew's food. The owners saw it as a way of saving wastage and therefore money.

Built by Herd and Mackenzie at their Peterhead yard, she was fitted with all the latest electronic devices of the time, including an echo sounder.

The Valafell

It was in May 1952 that the Grimsby trawler *Valafell* sailed into the record books — when she was arrested by the Russians for alleged illegal fishing. The detention was to cause a stir and provide an uncomfortable 12 days for the skipper and the 18-man crew of the vessel. It was to finish with a small financial penalty on the ship and rebellion by some of her crew members. It was on 12 May 1952 that the *Evening Telegraph* carried the headline: "Russians Arrest Grimsby Trawler."

That was the trawler *Valafell*, owned by Consolidated Fisheries. The report told how the vessel was arrested and was last seen in the early hours steaming eastward under escort by two Russian naval vessels. Mr J V Chatburn, who was then secretary to the Grimsby Fishing Vessel Owners' Mutual Insurance and Protecting Co Ltd, told of the arrest. The *Valafell* had been fishing four miles north-east of Vaida Bay off the North Russian coast.

Silence

She sailed from Grimsby on 23 April under the command of Skipper Jimmy Hobson, who had previously been skipper of the *Northern Spray*. Three days after her arrest there was still no news of the *Valafell* — and that silence, and frustrating and disturbing lack of information was to continue until 22 May. Then it was learned that the trawler had been fined 300 roubles (around £27 at that time) and released. A brief telegram received by her owners said the vessel was heading westward. It was assumed she had been held at Murmansk, but whether her catch had been disposed of and she had taken fresh ice aboard was not known. But for the *Valafell* the problems were far from over. Six days after news of her release came a report that five of her crewmen had been arrested in the Northern Norwegian port of Honingsvaag and accused by the skipper of refusing to return to the fishing grounds.

The trawler sailed for the White Sea fishing grounds at 5.30 pm that day with five Norwegians replacing the arrested Grimsby crewmen. It was on 16 June 1952 that the *Valafell* finally returned to Grimsby — and the crew immediately claimed they had been outside the Russian limits when arrested by the Soviet gunboat. Russian charts, however, showed her to have been inside their territorial waters. Ironically, despite her 55 days away, the *Valafell* was third vessel to berth. There was a new rule that ships with the shortest trips should be allowed to land first and this kept the trawler out in the river for 36 hours. A few days later, Skipper Hobson was prepared to tell his story of the arrest and subsequent treatment by the Russians. The *Valafell* had been taken to a small fishing port named Port Vladimir and although the crew did not get chance to step on to Russian soil they had ample opportunity to see what went on ashore.

Skipper Hobson spoke of the efficiency of the Russian interrogators who would ask the same question in three different ways. If the three replies were consistent they were satisfied and went on to something else. He and the crew were interrogated for as long as four or five hours at a time, but were allowed cigarettes and tea to drink.

The trawler had been required to move from the buoys in the harbour up to the quayside for water and was berthed at the side of a fish factory. Skipper Hobson said at the time: "The women workers did not give us a very friendly reception but I won't go any further than that. One man who seemed to be drunk waved his arms at us. He was soon picked up by the Russian soldiers who hustled him away without standing on ceremony." He said how amazed he and his crew had been at the conditions under which the women were

74. The Valafell pictured in northern waters.

working.

He spoke of clothing being in tatters and the women doing heavy manual work, pulling barrows laden with fish and moving casks about. Buildings were dilapidated and one which housed 18 families had a row of 20 broken windows most of which were boarded up.

Skipper Hobson also had words about the food. "I asked for some stores, meat, sugar, butter and potatoes which were all very expensive. The meat, for example, which cost about 14 shillings a pound, was dreadful stuff. They had no fresh meat to offer at all and what we got was from the Army's stores, rather like inferior quality stewed steak in a watery gravy. The other stores were not too bad but still way behind our idea of quality in food."

But despite everything, Skipper Hobson was prepared to concede that his compulsory holiday in Russia had not been as bad as had been expected. "We were treated fairly and with scrupulous courtesy. But the Russians made it very clear that deliberate poaching in Russian territorial waters would be treated as a serious offence, although they accepted my explanations that we were genuinely outside according to British charts," he recounted.

One man who remembered those days in Russia very well was Mr Mark Norman. A deckhand on the *Valafell*, he recalled: "We were gutting fish and the skipper had turned in. The first thing we knew was when the Russians were climbing over the rails with their bayonets fixed. They took us to Port Vladimir which was about 30 miles from Murmansk. When we arrived there it was like sailing into a big mountain. It opened out into a big bay once you got through. I remember asking one of the lads if he had heard the big bang. When he asked me what big bang, I said it was the sound of the Iron Curtain coming down!" Although the Russian guards remained very proper, Mr Norman did manage to get on friendly terms with one of them whom he christened Tojo.

"He used to try to read all our papers. When we were leaving I said I wanted something to remember him by. So he pulled off his cap badge and gave it to me. I gave him my Merchant Navy badge in return," said Mr Norman. He too had memories of the food on offer. "We had not had anything for a few days. And then they came up with this Yak meat and sweet potatoes! And I think they charged us about £153 for that," he grinned.

Tangle

The *Valafell*'s career after the Russian episode was pretty straightforward, although she tangled with the Icelanders in July 1955. She was arrested and taken into Akjureyri on the northern coast of Iceland for allegedly fishing within the territorial limits. Skipper on that occasion was Mr Arthur Bruce. The trawler was eventually fined 74,000 kironer (£1,600) for the alleged offence. There was a further incident in disputed Icelandic waters in February 1959 when reports said that two British destroyers, the *Agincourt* and *Corunna*, had intervened to prevent the gunboat *Thor* from arresting the *Valafell*. Britain and Iceland were at that time disputing an area between 4 and 12 miles from the Icelandic coast.

But what of the *Valafell* herself?

She was built by Cochrane and Son in Selby in 1942 and engined by Amos and Smith. Initially the Admiralty "Fish" class *Bream*, she was sold to Consols of Grimsby in 1946 and renamed.

Mr Harry Hutson, of Little Michael Street, Grimsby, who sailed on her as radio operator in the early Fifties, recalled she was a very bad sea ship, heavy on coal at full speeds, but with very good lines. She had iron decks from midships aft.

"My recollection of this class of ship was that they were the only trawlers out of Grimsby to carry two echo sounders for the specific purpose of measuring the depth of water both under and over the ship. They should have had a bung for the funnel too!" said Mr Hutson.

The *Valafell* was eventually scrapped in the late Fifties.

The Victory

The Grimsby freezer trawler *Victory* was less than ten years old when she met a dramatic end, engulfed by fire off the north Russian coast. For some time the Russians remained tight-lipped about the trawler's fate and the vessel was even raised in a discussion about the possibility of spies sailing aboard such fishing vessels. May Day became Mayday when on 1 May 1974 the 23 crew had to abandon the blazing trawler as fire threatened to envelop her engine room. The blaze was so fierce at one stage that the crew of the 1,200-ton freezer trawler were unable to control it. Her skipper, Mr Wally Wilson, who was then aged 36, ordered every man off and the entire crew was picked up unharmed by the Hull Freezer trawler *Kurd*, which had the *Victory* under tow. Reports at the time said the trawler was under tow by a Russian destroyer and believed to be heading for the big Soviet naval base of Murmansk. It was the second time in 24 hours fire had broken out on the *Victory*.

Engine Room

The drama had begun earlier in the day when the crew were called on to fight a fire in the engine room. They managed to bring that outbreak under control but in doing so used up a large amount of their carbon dioxide fire-fighting material. But while the battle was going on the *Kurd* — a sister ship of the ill-fated *Gaul*, had the *Victory* under tow to a Norwegian port. Then at about 5 pm, as slow progress towards safety was still being made, the second and devastating fire struck. Once again it was in the engine room and once again the crew responded. They made a brave attempt to fight the outbreak but very quickly had to admit it was a hopeless task. As the fire got a hold it threatened to sweep through the entire vessel and two fire-fighting tugs, one a Norwegian and the other from a Russian port, raced to the scene.

Dropped Tow

The *Kurd*, aware of the emergency, dropped her tow and turned back to rescue the *Victory*'s crew. The two firetugs suddenly arrived on the scene and started to damp down the fire.

Later one of them was to take the *Victory* in tow. Immediately her owners, British United Trawlers, began to try and contact the Soviet authorities. The crew were taken to Honingsvaag in Norway where arrangements were made to fly them home. Reports suggested the *Victory* was still burning as she was towed away from the scene. Two days later the whereabouts of the fire-gutted trawler remained a mystery.

Although it was believed she was in a Russian port BUT had been unable to get an answer from the Russian authorities. A spokesman told the *Evening Telegraph* at the time: "We have heard nothing and inquiries have been placed in the hands of the Ministry of Agriculture because their officials are better able to contact the Russians."

Sprayed Oil

A spokesman at the Ministry said: "It was a May Day holiday in Russia and that is probably why there is a delay in obtaining information." It was learned the original fire had broken out while the vessel was fishing in the White Sea when a fuel line burst and sprayed oil over the engine room. The second fire was so severe it began to melt the bridge. On 6 May the news was confirmed that the *Victory* was, as suspected, tied up in the Russian port of Murmansk. Back in Grimsby further details of the terrifying fire became clear.

The mate, Mr Phil McCarthy, said it was a miracle the crew had survived the inferno. Things were so bad in fact that Norwegian radio put out reports that the trawler had sunk.

Melted Deck

Mr McCarthy told waiting reporters: "It was an absolute inferno. When we abandoned her the ship was burning from stem to stern and the bridge deck started to melt. It is a miracle that we are all alive. The ship could have blown up."

The second blaze was thought to have started in the refrigeration room. The vessel was so hot that water from two Russian gunboats turned into steam as soon as it made contact. Mr McCarthy said that at one point it was feared an engineer was trapped in the engine room.

"I was just about to try to go in and get him when I was told he had got out through an escape hatch. There was nothing we could do about the second fire," he said. There were around 200 tons of fish on board at the time of the fire.

Survey Flight

Meanwhile a BUT official and a representative of the underwriters, UK Trawlers Mutual Insurance Company, were geared up to fly to Russia to survey the damage and deal with any salvage claim. That inspection would determine whether the trawler should be repaired and brought home. But it was almost three months before the Russians broke their silence over the fate of the ship. Although the Soviet authorities had sent a message confirming the trawler was in Murmansk, tied up and badly damaged, there had been no further information. But then, at the end of September, the Russians told the insurers the vessel could be inspected. Manager of the insurance company, Mr Bill Taylor, made the trip and came back with a report that the *Victory* was so badly damaged that she was considered to be a write-off. She was lying on her starboard side with about one-third showing at low water level.

75. The shape of the 60s — the freezer trawler Victory. She was abandoned after a serious fire in 1976.

BLOATER PASTE

4 herrings
1/4 lb of butter
2 tablespoons of Anchovy sauce
mixed spice to taste

Simmer herrings half an hour in boiling water, then remove skin and bones. Chop the fish and all hard roes, melt the butter, and mix well with the other ingredients. Pound in a mortar and put into jars.

Friendliness

Mr Taylor who had the assistance of BUT's superintendent engineer, Mr J J Ewert, in inspecting the vessel, spoke later of the friendliness of his Russian hosts. He said at the time:

"They have come in for a good deal of criticism and they are upset about it. I think it is about time somebody spoke out in their favour. They were really very kind to us," said Mr Taylor. The *Victory*'s experiences came to the forefront again when the question of "spies" sailing aboard trawlers was raised. Navy Minister of the time, Mr Frank Judd, confirmed that Royal Navy personnel did sometimes sail on British trawlers. Hull East MP, Mr John Prescott, expressed concern about the safety of crewmen in such circumstances. And he pledged to ask questions about the *Victory* in view of the fact she had been held for so long without her owners being allowed to see her.

Then in November 1974 came the news that the trawler, which cost £750,000 to build, had finally been written off.

Tragic End

It was a tragic end for a trawler which had started her career in a blaze of glory. Built in Aberdeen by John Lewis and Sons Ltd, she was described by that yard as the finest vessel they had ever built.

At the time she was the first all-freezing trawler to join Associated Fisheries' Grimsby fleet working through Northern Trawlers. Great play was made at the time around the fact she was able to stay at sea for 50 days and had refrigerated fish rooms with a capacity of more than 500 tons of blocks of frozen fish.

The crew's facilities included a film room and a library. She was skippered on her maiden voyage by Mr Bernard "Bunny" Newton. And she eventually docked at Grimsby with a 540-ton catch — the largest ever achieved by a British freezer trawler — which would provide enough fish for about 2,300,000 meals.

New Links

When she was new, links were forged between her and the Trafalgar veteran HMS *Victory*. Lt Cmdr C W Whittington, captain of HMS *Victory*, came to Grimsby for a luncheon at the Royal Hotel. And he told the guests: "HMS *Victory* belongs not to the Navy but to the nation — and to the sea in particular.

"We are sure that this new *Victory* with all her modern equipment and advances will be a fitting symbol in memory of the many thousands of men who have given their lives to seeing that British seamen and British ships are amongst the finest in the world."

The Equerry

The trawler *Equerry* left Grimsby for the White Sea fishing grounds on 8 September 1952 — but it was 45 days before she returned after being held by the Russians. And if it had not been for another Grimsby vessel, the fate of the trawler might not have been known for much longer.

As it was, the trawler *Serron* saw the *Equerry* being escorted by a Russian gunboat and managed to get a message back to Grimsby. It was 1.30 am on the morning of 21 September 1952 that the gunboat arrested the vessel for allegedly illegally fishing along the Murmansk coast. Immediately the British Ambassador in Moscow, Sir A D F Gascoigne, was instructed by the Foreign Office to make inquiries of the Russian government about the incident.

A short radio message from the *Serron* had been sent back to Grimsby stating: "Equerry sighted steaming eastwards along the north coast of Russia escorted by gunboat." That was the only indication of her arrest. The Russians themselves said nothing in the first instance.

Cigarettes

For her skipper, Mr William Henry Wilson, it was the second time he had been in Russian custody. He was a deckhand with the *York City* in 1938 when she was detained by the Russians for alleged illegal fishing. After that incident he told how they had been well treated by their captors, who had given them cigarettes. On his very next voyage in the *York City* the vessel went on the rocks off the Norwegian coast and Mr Wilson, along with other members of the crew, was in the water for a considerable time before being rescued. That incident was to cause the postponement of his wedding for two weeks.

76. The Equerry pictured in the early 50s. A former Hull trawler, she came to Grimsby in 1937 and was scrapped in 1958.

HALIBUT COLLOPS

4 lbs halibut (slices)
1 teaspoonful of pepper and ginger
2 teaspoonfuls chopped onions or parsley
2 teaspoonfuls of salt
2 ozs dripping
2 ozs flour
1 pint milk

Sprinkle slices with salt, pepper, ginger and chopped onions. Put them into a pie dish with the dripping, and pour over them a sauce made by boiling the flour and milk together until smooth. Bake for half an hour in a moderate oven, and send to the table with parsley strewed over.

Immediately after the arrest of the *Equerry* her owners, the Loyal Steam Fishing Company, promised to let relatives know as soon as they had more information.

Fined

But it was over a week before the news came through that the vessel had been released by the Russians. She had been fined 300 roubles, which was the equivalent of around £27 at the time. Information from Moscow said the vessel had been released after the fine had been paid by the British embassy. The Russian Foreign Ministry said the trawler had been charged with illegal fishing in territorial waters 2.4 miles off the Russian coast in the Barents Sea. Confiscation of some of the vessel's catch had also been ordered by the Soviet court. The fine was the same as that imposed on the Grimsby trawler *Valafell*, which had faced a similar charge some months earlier.

The *Equerry* left Russia and headed for Harstad in Norway, where one of the first things Skipper Wilson did was to phone his wife back home in Colin Avenue, Grimsby. Mrs Wilson told an *Evening Telegraph* reporter at the time: "He said he and the crew were well cared for while they were in Russia. He expected to be leaving Harstad for the fishing grounds within 24 hours and to be back in Grimsby in about 17 days."

Sealed

It was revealed then that armed Russian guards had been put aboard the *Equerry* while she was detained, but the skipper and crew had been treated well. The guards had sealed the radio set, making it impossible for the radio operator to report home what had happened. However, the Russians had provided whatever supplies the vessel needed. Coal and water were put aboard and medical help provided when needed. The crew wer not allowed ashore at all during their capture. It was 21 October 1952 when the *Equerry* slipped through the lock-gates into the Fish docks at the end of her marathon voyage.

The *Evening Telegraph* recorded that the cheer could be heard all over the docks estate as the trawler was spotted. The cheers went up again as the vessel slid through the swing bridge cutting and again as she nosed in to tie up at the west wall, where relatives and friends of the crew together with a few officials were waiting to greet her.

Immediately lumpers went to work to land 1,550 kits of White Sea fish the trawler had caught after leaving Harstad. And the crew told of their enforced stay in Russian waters. The cook, Mr Bill Akins, who lived in Kingsley Grove, Nunthorpe, told waiting reporters that although they could not go ashore they had been treated very well.

"I had a tooth extracted by a Russian woman dentist. I was not feeling well owing to violent toothache. She came aboard and had a look at it and told me I had an abcess on the gum close to the tooth. She took it out without using an anaesthetic and I did not feel a thing. She was a good dentist.

"Later she gave me some tablets which she said would keep out the cold. She also gave me a box of 50 Russian cigarettes — the boys call them Ragman's Trumpets because of the long filter."

Polite

Third hand Mr George Lawn was even more outspoken in his praise of the Russians. He told reporters:

"I have been in every country in the world save New Zealand and Australia, and I can honestly say that I have not had better treatment anywhere. An officer came on board to interrogate us. He was very polite and asked me whether I lived in a house in England. Then he asked about housing conditions and to which political party I belonged. Most of us said we did not belong to any party since we did not have the time. We spent the time in Vladimir teaching the Russian guards knots and splices."

Friends

Chief engineer Mr Jack Berry, who lived in New Holland, told newsmen: "I do not think the Russians are as bad as some people would like to make out. The captain of the coastal security boat which arrested us was very polite and very helpful. He seemed very sorry to be arresting us. We were interrogated and I was asked about the type of school I had attended and my political party. They gave us plenty of cigarettes but they would not accept any of ours. I made friends with one of the guards whose name was Sascha. He was always very happy and smiling and the crew nicknamed him Laughing Boy."

Skipper Wilson remembered the incident vividly. "I was turned in at the time after a few days fishing. There was no doubt that we had gone inside the limit," he recalled.

"It was a bit of a shaky experience because there had been a warning from the Russians that any trawler skipper caught illegally fishing could be sent to labour camps. But I think they appreciated that I was telling them the absolute truth," said Skipper Wilson.

When the *Equerry* finally arrived back in Grimsby after her 45 day trip, Mr Wilson had to go before a disciplinary committee." Although I had not been at the wheel at the time I got three months suspension, which was equivalent to a £1,000 fine at the time," he recalled.

Skipper Wilson had kind words for the *Equerry* too. "She was a very good sea ship and a very good fishing ship. I certainly caught some fish in her." Mr Jim Mann, was just 22 at the time of the incident. "But I remember it as though it was yesterday," he said. He told how the gunboat came alongside at around 1.30 am and armed guards were put aboard the trawler. They went straight up to the wireless room to stop us getting any messages out." He remembered that after the long trip the *Equerry* had grossed £7,550 for her catch.

"The drama didn't end in Russia either. On the way back we ran out of coal just about at Spurn. We had to burn anything we could to help us make it to the dock. I often wonder what would have happened if the *Serron* had not spotted us and passed the message on that we had been captured," said Mr Mann.

Flooded

Less than two years later the *Equerry* was in trouble of a different kind. She had sailed from Grimsby in January 1954 with a crew of 17 under the command of Skipper R Smith, a Hull man. On 24 January she radioed to say she was trying to make Aberdeen with her boiler tubes leaking badly. At 11.38 am the next day came the dramatic message:

"Four miles east south east of Buchanness, require immediate assistance, stokehold flooded." The Grimsby trawler *Northern Sun* went to her assistance and eventually managed to take her in tow. Both the Peterhead and Fraserburgh lifeboats were launched, but returned when it was learned the *Northern Sun* had arrived on the scene.

The *Equerry* eventually made Aberdeen for repairs. Sadly, she was later scrapped. She had been built in Beverley in 1929.

The Etruria

The *Etruria* hit the headlines and brought questions in the House of Commons when she was arrested by the Russians on 1 May 1950. The trawler was held for ten days under an armed guard, but was eventually released after much haggling between the respective authorities and the payment of a £30 fine.

Rumours of the arrest were rife before it was officially confirmed. That

FILLETS OF COD

2 slices of cod, cut rather thick
Savoury batter

Cut the cod into little round fillets, dip them in batter and fry a light brown in deep hot fat. Drain well and arrange the fillets in a circle, garnish with fried parsley.

Batter:
Method:- Put 4 oz of flour in a bowl with a pinch of salt and a gill of lukewarm water, add two tablespoons of salads oil. Beat the whites of two eggs to a stiff froth, and stir them in just before the batter is required.

confirmation came on 3 May when the vessel's owners, the Standard Steam Fishing Company, reported that the *Etruria* had been boarded and taken into Murmansk.

The *Etruria* had managed to get out a brief radio message which was picked up by a Hull trawler. The message said the 187-ton vessel had been boarded and ordered to stop. The vessel had sailed from Grimsby on 18 April bound for the White Sea fishing grounds under the command of Skipper Jim Chapman. At the time it was known that several British trawlers had been chased by Russian patrol boats but none had been detained. News of the arrest for alleged illegal fishing within three miles of the Russian coast brought rapid diplomatic activity.

The Foreign Office sent instructions to the British Embassy in Moscow asking for the vessel's immediate release. The Fisheries Ministry also took up the case.

The *Etruria* was carrying a 21-man crew. As well as Skipper Chapman it included mate Mr J Mann of Hull; first engineer C Turrell of Park Street, Grimsby; second engineer Mr C Mayes of Norwich; and third hand Mr Albert Duffin of Cleethorpes.

Mr John Paterson,, was one of the three trimmers aboard her. He recalled that he had been below when the boarding occurred.

"We were ordered to haul our gear. There was a guard on the forecastle, one in the engine room and two on the bridge. They were armed with rifles," said Mr Paterson.

The first thing the Russians did was to order the wireless operator Mr Joe Fleet out of the wireless room and they closed the equipment down. The vessel was ordered to follow the American-built gunboat into Murmansk and tie up at the quay.

"When they let us go ashore we could only walk about the length of the trawler. One thing I noticed were the British-built cranes on the quayside. They must have been there from the war," said Mr Paterson.

The *Etruria* was thoroughly searched to make sure there were no cameras aboard and each member of the crew was questioned individually by their Russian captors.

"A man came aboard in a green uniform and we were all taken individually into the skipper's cabin and questioned.

They asked where we had been and if we belonged to the Labour Party or the Communist Party," said Mr Paterson. A catch of cod was taken off the trawler by the Russians but they left the crew with some 140 kits of plaice for food.

"We had our own food, of course. The guards would not eat anything. They would only drink water," remembered Mr Paterson.

But on the whole the Russians looked after their charges well.

"They were really decent. There was no brutality or anything like that. In fact we became quite chummy in the end," said Mr Paterson. But all the time they were uncertain how long they were going to be held or what moves were being made back home to bring about their release. Mr Cyril Duffin,whose late father Albert was third hand, related some of the stories about the 'capture' his father told.

"He said the guards used to have them on deck for fresh air. And the Russians used to go crazy over the *Picture Post*. There were copies on board," said Mr Duffin.

His father "celebrated" his 42nd birthday during the vessel's detention.

"He brought back three or four Russian cigarettes. They were like a full-length fag but three quarters of it was a cardboard tube with just a dog end stuck in it," said Mr Duffin.

As the *Etruria* lay in Murmansk harbour, 2,000 miles away the Commons was hearing of her arrest. Mr Ernest Davies, Under Secretary at the Foreign Office, made a statement in the House about the incident. With no radio contact available with the *Etruria* everything had to be done through diplomatic channels.

Experts began examining the provisions of the Anglo-Soviet fishing agreement of 1930 which gave British trawlers the right to fish within three miles of Russia's north-west coast. The view was that any interference with fishing vessels outside that three-mile limit would be a direct contravention of that agreement.

For days there was no further news of the trawler. Mr J V Chatburn, representing the owners, kept in close contact with the various Ministries. On 9 May it was reported that the Russians were willing to release the *Etruria* on condition that the Grimsby owners paid a fine.

The following day the British Government revealed its intention to challenge the legality of the Russians' action. Sir David Kelly, British Ambassador in Moscow, sought a meeting with the Soviet Deputy Foreign Minister Mr Gromyko. And Hull skipper J W Hornsby of the trawler *Kingston Amber* came back with a first-hand report of the *Etruria*'s arrest.

He told how he had seen the vessel being escorted by the gunboat off the Murmansk coast. There were around five Hull and Grimsby vessels in the area at the time.

On 11 May the 300 roubles (£30 fine) was paid by the company after Mr Gromyko confirmed that that would secure the release of the trawler. At 2 am on 12 May Skipper Chapman sent a message home stating simply: "Released 11th, signed Chapman." But that eventful trip was not over yet. On the way home the *Etruria* was involved in a clash with the Norwegian fisheries protection vessel, *King Haakon VII*.

Mr Don Scales, another of the *Etruria*'s deckhands, recalled that when the

77. The Etruria.

> ***POTTED HERRINGS***
>
> *Take some herrings fresh, and clean them well but do not wash them, cut off the heads and fins and take the bones put, strew them over with salt and pepper, and a slice of onion nicely minced to each, roll them up tightly, pack them in a jar, and pour over them in the proportion of a pint of vinegar to two of water, with half an ounce of whole black pepper. Tie over the jar a piece of bladder or paper, and bake them in the oven for an hour. Take off the cover when they are cold, and pour over them a little cold vinegar and tie them up.*

vessel had first been arrested she was taken into a creek on the Murmansk coast — the site of a women's prison. The women used to have to work in the small fishing industry based on the creek.

"They used to march them down in a morning and then back at night," said Mr Scales.

He remembered too the clash with the Norwegian protection vessel.

"The Russians bought the cod from us but they did not want the plaice. When we got to Honningsvaag we asked if we could transfer the plaice onto a Hull trawler. I think they said no. But the skipper decided to go ahead anyway," said Mr Scales. The move was spotted by the authorities and the protection vessel came on the scene.

"We got a summons for that. The fish fetched about £600 but it was not enough to pay the fine," he said. Even that incident did not deter Skipper Chapman. Determined to get a trip in he fished close to the Norwegian coast, narrowly avoiding further detection. Eventually she got together a trip of 1,020 kits.

"The Russians told us to go straight back home but we went fishing instead," said Mr Scales.

Later the owners of the *Etruria* decided not to appeal against conviction and sentence for the Russian episode. It was agreed that the method adopted in fixing the position of the trawler was liable to error — although Skipper Chapman maintained he had not been within three miles of the Russian coast when arrested.

Crazy but Courageous

The *Etruria* was built in Beverley in 1930 for Jutland Amalgamated Trawlers Ltd of Hull, and originally named the *Lady Elsa*. She was bought by the Great Grimsby and East Coast S F Fishing Co Ltd in 1937. She was lengthened on the South Bank in 1939 to 160 feet. That was achieved by removing her straight stem and counter stern and replacing them with a raking bow and cruiser stern. That adaptation gave her more speed, but did not improve her as a "sea" ship

. One former crewman went so far as to describe her as a "dirty" ship constantly taking water.

Another skipper, Ernest Lovett, who took her in the early Fifties, said: "She used to take these violent lists. She was crazy.

He first sailed her as mate under Skipper Fred Webb — known to the crew as "Captain Lash". "He was a tough guy but a nice fella," said Skipper Lovett.

On 18 December 1939, the Etruria was attacked by a German aircraft while on her way to the fishing grounds. She received a direct bomb hit on forecastle. Three members of the crew who were sheltering in the forecastle were killed and another injured.

The trawler was extensively damaged. Around 15 bombs were dropped and the ship was machine-gunned.However, she was able to reach a northern port safely.

The vessel served with the Navy — taking part in the Dunkirk evacuation — from May 1940 until February 1946 as a boom defence vessel under her own name.

On 9 December 1940 the trawler had her first tangle with Norwegian gunboats. She was arrested for illegal fishing and escorted to Hammerfest, where Skipper Chapman was ordered to pay penalties totalling £2,000. She had been stopped six nautical miles north west of Nordkyn lighthouse.

Blizzard Collision

Only a few weeks later both engineers of the vessel, Mr J W Stewart and Mr George Blackett, had to be dragged from the engine room and given medical treatment after trying to free bilge pumps in heavy seas. After they had been crouched at their pumps for a considerable time, Mr Stewart was struck on the arm by a piece of falling machinery, while Mr Blackett got cramp. Both were treated at hospital in Tynemouth.

In March 1950 the *Etruria* was in trouble again — in collision with the Hull trawler *White Flower* during a blizzard off Hammerfest. Damage to the trawler was slight — one plate dented and the vessel continued her journey home. The *White Flower*, on the other hand, was heavily damaged in the bow but reached Hammerfest without assistance.

Mr Jack Everett, was a deckie/learner aboard the *Etruria* in the early Fifties.

He recalled one nightmare of a trip when the Russians this time came to the assistance of the Grimsby crew — but had their advice ignored. The trawler was operating off the Russian coast. "We had just about finished our trip and the weather was appalling. We had only got about 300 kits. Then the weather started to clear.

"Then the Russians came over to us. They told us to get gear up and get out of the area because the weather was going to be really bad. We took no notice. We were all on the deck gutting plaice. The sky took on a pale, yellowy colour and the trawler began freezing up. It was so cold that we could not get our breath. Some of the older men on board were practically keeling over," said Mr Everett.

The plaice were freezing as the men tried to gut them. When an attempt was made to start a winch, the drive shaft shattered like glass because of the intense cold.

"They were the worst conditions I have ever known in my life. We had to go into Vardo in the end," Mr Everett added.

Cosy Corner

The aforementioned Skipper Chapman was a character in his own right and well known to Grimsby freelance journalist Charles Ekberg. He remembered him as a heavily-built red faced man who was a regular customer in the old exclusive gent's room at the Pestle and Mortar public house in the Old Market Place. His pals were fish merchant Joe Parker, cafe owner Perch Noble, clothier Charles Skeffington, seaman Bill Hartshorne and bookies' runner Mr Stafford.

"These chaps occupied one corner of the room by the open fire, and this was known as the House of Commons," said Mr Ekberg.

He recalled that Skipper Chapman attended every morning and evening session at the pub while he was in dock.

"He, Joe and Percy sported big fur hats — those with brims — and Chapman presented them, though whether he got them in Russia I don't know."

Very Generous

He recalled that Skipper Chapman and Mr Parker were both very generous. Both were in the habit of saying to hard-up and newly married journalist Charles Ekberg: "Go in the back of the car and you will find a present."

"There was usually a piece of beef or a bass of fish," remembered Mr Ekberg. He said that Skipper Chapman had been sworn to secrecy over the Russian incident.

"Those P & M regulars always occupied the same seats and Chapman once threatened to punch me because I deliberately went into his seat just for the hell of it.

"I lost sight of Jim in the 1950s, though I rang him late in 1958 when I was publishing a magazine called *Humber Industry* for some information I needed. He was in Hull then.

"I remember he did not come into a room — he burst in — and as the doors to the P & M were a bit close together, he usually made quite an entrance," he added.

The Brandur

It took Skipper Bunny Newton just one incident aboard the Grimsby trawler *Brandur* to become the port's most famous skipper of all time. For when you are arrested by the Icelandics for illegal fishing and then make a run for it — taking two Icelandic policemen with you — the whole world sits up and takes notice!

And that's just what happened in April 1967, and it's a story that is just as amazing today as it was then. It also marked another chapter in the history of one of Grimsby's best loved trawlers — for the *Brandur* had seen previous service from the port as the *Boston Fury*.

She was sold to Faroese owners and became the *Fiskanes* but later came back to Britain. She went to work from Hull but in 1966 she returned to fish from Grimsby as the *Brandur*, with her former owners Boston Deep Sea Fisheries as managers.

The first news that anything unusual had happened on that fateful trip to the Icelandic fishing grounds came on 25 April 1967, when reports reached Grimsby saying the *Brandur* had been arrested for alleged illegal fishing. Those reports said the *Brandur* had been spotted by a coastguard plane three and a half nautical miles off Eldey on the south west coast of Iceland. It was said that when the aircraft called the trawler by radio she headed for the open sea.

That most famous of Icelandic gunboats, *Thor*, was called up and arrested the trawler. Two days later a spokesman for the vessel's managers reported that Skipper Newton had been in court until 11 pm the previous night "and must be making a fight of it."

The case seemed to be following the normal pattern of similar ones which had gone before — until 29 April. Then the whole port of Grimsby was stunned and amazed at the news that Skipper Newton had broken out of Reykjavik Harbour and made a run for home.

A Dash

As if that wasn't enough, he had made the dash for freedom with two Icelandic policemen still aboard! But just 11 hours later Skipper Newton and his crew were back in custody. The *Brandur* had been stopped 43 miles off Iceland.

She had painted a new number on her side, replacing the original GY111 with H52 when she slipped the harbour. A coastguard plane was sent up to hunt the trawler and a sloop was also diverted. It had orders to use force, if necessary, to arrest her — inside or outside Icelandic waters. The disappearance of the *Brandur* was discovered early that morning when two policemen went down to the harbour to relieve their colleagues who had been on guard on the trawler all night.

The *Brandur*, which had been moored at the outermost quay, had gone — and with her the two guards. She had slipped out of the harbour at 1 am. Earlier the court had heard that the *Brandur* had been arrested when she was spotted fishing inside Iceland's 12-mile fishing limit.

Skipper Newton, who pleaded not guilty, agreed the trawler had been inside the limit but denied she had been fishing. He argued that a big boulder had been caught in the trawl. The 23-man crew thought at first it might be a wartime mine and as they were hauling it gingerly aboard, the trawler drifted inside the limit

. Skipper Newton tried to make it back to Grimsby because he was annoyed with the legal proceeding dragging on. Back in Reykjavik Judge Armann Kristinsson ruled that the skipper should be kept in custody for the length of the case, or 30 days. There was a further delay when May Day, a national holiday halted the court proceedings.

Meanwhile in Grimsby, Mr F B Parkes, managing director of Boston's, made a formal protest to the Foreign Office over the way the charge had been handled.

Gunpoint

He said he considered it most unreasonable, especially when the company had offered a bond of between £5,000 and £6,000 to cover any likely fine. And they were annoyed too, that the Icelanders seemed determined to ignore the fact that Skipper Newton had the stone he had caught in his net on board the ship.

78. Grimsby trawler the Brandur.

On the night of 1 May Skipper Newton telephoned his wife and revealed that he had been held at gunpoint when he was re-arrested. There were further problems just 24 hours later when fire swept though the *Brandur* as she lay in Reykjavik harbour.

Several of the crew had to be taken off by police while firemen fought the outbreak for about 40 minutes.

The fire, which was believed to have started in the boiler room or the paint store, gutted a two-man berth. Other berths were flooded by water from the hoses.

The crewmen spent the night in a sailors' home but were allowed back on the trawler the following day. Skipper Newton faced yet another delay — with another Icelandic public holiday for Ascension Day, getting in the way of the hearing. By this time Boston's had given up any hopes of saving the 1,000 or so kits of fish which were rotting on board. And they were frustrated and angry that the Icelanders would still not release the trawler.

Skipper Newton gave an interview to Matthias Johannessen, the then editor of the Icelandic daily newspaper Morganhladid. He stressed that no harm had been meant to the two Icelandic policemen and that in fact one had told him he had not stopped him leaving the port because he did not regard Skipper Newton as a criminal.

Knife

And he told the interviewer: "Then the policeman took a knife from his belt, concealed by his jacket, and handed it to me saying 'Keep it as souvenir.'

79. A wave from the Skipper of the Brandur.

We both laughed. I took the knife but then returned it to the policeman. It had been a friendly gesture on his part, a gesture I shall never forget."

Back in court Skipper Newton again denied having used any violence against the two officers but admitted he had locked them up in a cabin. But eventually Skipper Newton was found guilty of trying to escape with his arrested ship and obstructing the policemen with threats. For that he was given a three months prison sentence. He was also fined 300,000 crowns — about £2,400 — for fishing within Iceland's 12-mile limit. He was freed, however, when the vessel's owners immediately put up a £100,000 bond pending appeal. Then came the problem of getting the vessel and its catch home. Initially Boston's ordered Skipper Newton to head for home because it seemed landing labour was not available to get the fish ashore in Iceland.

The *Brandur* left Reykjavik at 10 pm on 6 May. There was a move to divert him back to another Icelandic port to land but eventually Boston's reaffirmed the decision to bring him back to Grimsby. However, on 9 May she pulled into Aberdeen and landed her catch, grossing £2,500. Only three boxes of haddock were condemned by the port health officials although the fish was said to be of poor quality. But the eventful trip was not over yet.

Nine crewmen at first refused to sail with the ship from Aberdeen because they claimed there was no food aboard. But they were eventually persuaded by Skipper Newton and the *Brandur* left on the last leg of her journey. On 10 May 1967 the trawler made an undramatic entry into Grimsby Fish Docks and Skipper Newton said simply: "I want to get back to sea as soon as I can."

Shock

And he was soon to get his wish.

A few days later the *Brandur*, cleaned up, left for the fishing grounds with Skipper Newton again in charge. Most of the crew involved in the incident also rejoined her.

But it was some months before the appeal court met in Iceland to hear Skipper Newton's case — and when it did there was a shock decision. They doubled the prison sentence to six months and increased the fine to just over £2,500.

Skipper Newton was radioed on board the trawler *Oratava* and told to avoid the Icelandic fishing grounds. He headed for the Faroes. The legal wrangling went on. And then on 19 December 1968 came the final scene in the long running drama.

Skipper Newton heard that he had been granted a free pardon by the Icelandic authorities. It was one of a number of free pardons granted on 1 December, the Icelandic Day of Independence. The *Brandur* on the other hand, was not so lucky.

She had left Grimsby on 25 April for a Clydeside scrapyard. The vessel had become uneconomical to operate and had been laid up for some months.

The story has a happy ending. Skipper Newton stayed away from Iceland for 15 years but returned there in March 1982 — to be greeted by one of the policemen he had locked up.

Mr Hilmar Porbjornsson had risen through the ranks to become deputy sheriff of Reykjavik. Skipper Newton was treated to lunch in the new police station — a reception much better than he got all those years before.

FISH CAKES

1 lb of cold fish
1lb of potatoes
1 teaspoon of milk
1/2 oz of butter
Yolk of 1 egg

Heat butter, and mix ingredients together. Roll into balls, flatten, dip in egg and breadcrumbs. Fry in boiling fat for 3 minutes.

RANTER'S WHARF

On Ranter's Wharf the sun
went sailing down
Like an old square — rigger
bound for sea once more;
And in the murmur of the
evening tide
I heard a small voice crying . .
. crying on the shore.

I found her weeping by the
water side
And the evening shadows like
a cloak she wore —
"Oh Betsy Walton is my name,
kind sir —
I'm here to seek my Johnny . .
. Johnny on the shore."

"My Johnny was a handsome
sailor - lad,
And I lost him in the gale of
'ninety four —
His vessel broken on the
midnight sand,
And here they found him
lying . . . lying on the shore."

"I watch the seasons come
and go, kind sir,
And I'm waiting still, for
what can I do more?
Sometimes I think my
Johnny's calling me ,
When I hear the seagulls
crying . . . crying on the
shore."

On Ranter's Wharf the tide
was turning now;
When the moon came through,
no silver girl I saw —
And was I dreaming, or a
drunken man —
When I heard a seagull crying
. . . crying on the shore.

John Conolly

"Ranter's Wharf" is a dockside alley off Grimsby's Victoria Street. This song emerged from the traditional belief that the souls of drowned seamen are transmuted into seagulls.

Close to Home

The Algoma

Aground on the rocks near Spurn Point the Grimsby trawler *Algoma* was the scene of one of the strangest birthday parties ever seen. For as huge waves battered the vessel the nine men on board clung on where they could and drank the skipper's health in tea! And though they were in great danger the crew managed to also eat the birthday cake which had been made for him. Eventually the men were hauled to safety 120ft up towering cliffs.

It was on 23 February 1936 that the *Algoma* actually grounded in fog under the cliffs at Dimlington, a few miles north of Spurn. It was skipper G Jack's birthday — hence the celebrations. The ship keeled over to starboard and that put the crew in real peril. She was helpless under the cliffs with sea washing over her and the crew huddled in the bows waiting for help. The Holmpton Rocket Brigade which had struggled to the scene through rain and wind finally succeeded in firing a line over the vessel and the men were hauled to safety in the breeches buoy.

No Wine

By then the crew had had its celebration. Although there was no wine to toast the skipper, the third hand, W Meadows of Wood Street, Grimsby, volunteered to try to make his way along the wave-swept deck to the galley to make a pot of tea. When he returned with the tea and the birthday cake which had been made before the ship ran aground, the fishermen joined in the celebration when the toast was "The Skipper".

The *Algoma*, which had been built in 1899 and was owned by Alfred Bannister (Trawlers) Ltd, had been homeward bound from the fishing grounds in the early hours of Sunday morning. She ran aground on the mud and sand beneath the cliffs on the Yorkshire coast during fog and rain. Rockets were fired and flares were lit but it was not until three hours later that there came an answering flash from the shore. At daybreak the Holmpton Brigade arrived with their breeches buoy and the Humber lifeboat also arrived on the scene. The men on the trawler decided the breeches buoy was the best way of leaving the ship and one by one they were pulled to safety. At low water the crew returned to the trawler, walking across the mud and sand and a warp was laid with bladders attached. Then the salvage tug arrived from Grimsby,

80, 81. ***opposite page:*** *Crewmen on board the Ephesian in the late 50s.*
82. ***left****: The Algoma ashore on the Yorkshire coast.*

picked up the bladders and made fast to the *Algoma* which was successfully refloated.

The trawler then returned to Grimsby under her own steam, arriving in time to land her catch for the market the following day.

On their return to Grimsby the men spoke to the *Evening Telegraph* of the grounding. Skipper Jack told a reporter: "We were returning home from a fishing voyage in the North Sea and on Sunday morning the weather was thick and rainy.

"We felt the ship lurch and the engines were put astern but the swell gradually worked her on to the beach.

"We fired rockets and showed flares but we could not get any answer until 6 am when we saw a morse message being flashed from the cliff top.

Ordeal

"They asked us if we wanted any assistance and we asked them to stand by until daylight.

"After daybreak the Spurn lifeboat arrived and we were taken ashore in the breeches buoy.

"After having something to eat at a farmhouse we returned to the ship and on Sunday afternoon we were refloated by the salvage tug from Grimsby."

The cook, Mr F Avison, told the *Evening Telegraph* at the time that it was the worst ordeal he had undergone in a lifetime of going to sea.

He said: "After the ship struck there were heavy seas running and these swept the ship from end to end. We came to the conclusion that the safest place was in the bows.

"We dare not go into the fo'c'stle for fear of being trapped there if the ship heeled over.

"We made the best of it. It was the skipper's birthday and I'd made a cake — no fancy icing or anything like that, just a plain cake — so we decided to eat it and the third hand fetched a pot of tea from the galley.

"We were sorry we hadn't any wireless because it would have brightened things up.

"We were all wet through because although we missed the full force of the

83. The crew of the Algoma back on board after their rescue.

seas, some of which swept over the wheelhouse, we could not get out of the way of them altogether."

Other crewmen told how it had been bitterly cold in the bows of the vessel. The men had tried to keep warm with a bit of fire on which they burned anything the galley could lay their hands on. One of the crew had a tin of peppermints which he handed round to help keep his colleagues warm. Maurice Newton, one of the deckhands, was just 17 at the time. He told how after the grounding the crew tried to launch the boat but it was broken up by the very heavy seas.

The life-saving company from Holmpton had to struggle through torrential rain to get to the scene. When the distress signals from the *Algoma* were seen the lifeboat was called out. Under Coxswain Robert Cross, *City of Bradford* made as fast as she could for the scene and she stood by while the Rocket Brigade fired their line over the stranded trawler. In fact the lifeboat had covered the nine miles from her base to the scene in just under an hour and she stood by until all the crew were safely landed.

Frantic

Algoma had run ashore around 2 am but after her position had been located by the life-saving company the waggon carrying apparatus became stuck in the mud in one of the fields over which it had to be taken. Frantic efforts followed to free it and eventually four horses managed to pull it free and dragged it another mile to reach the trawler. Chief coastguard at Holmpton, Mr W Harding, said they had not found the trawler until 4 am. After being pulled up the cliffs the crew was taken to nearby Easington and looked after by a representative of the Shipwrecked Mariners.

Coxswain Cross told reporters: "When we received the message relayed through Mablethorpe we launched at once. A heavy sea was running and as the wind dropped fog came on.

"The trawler was lying on her starboard side and we went alongside. She was being swept by heavy seas as the tide went out.

"When the life-saving company arrived they fired a rocket and line which went directly over the trawler and lifeboat."

Afterwards it was found that as a result of the breakers washing over the vessel her hold was partly flooded. The same weekend another Grimsby trawler, the *Flandre*, was also in trouble. The vessel, belonging to the Earl Steam Fishing Company, was making for Scalloway in the Shetlands with a new propeller for the Grimsby trawler *Louis Botha* which had stripped her original one.

The Deveron

It was a bleak winter's day as the Yorkshire vicar made his way out to the Grimsby trawler *Deveron*, stranded like a crippled seabird on the coast near Kilnsea. Struggling to the side of the vessel he spotted a member of the crew standing shivering on the deck. Cupping his hands about his mouth the vicar shouted encouragingly: "I am the local vicar. Is there anything I can do for you?"

The reply came back sharply: "Yes, pull this bugger off!" Such was the frustration felt by all concerned with the stranding of the vessel just around the corner from Spurn Point on 4 January 1949. Messages were flashed from the trawler that she had gone ashore near Kilnsea in a gale, blinded by driving sleet. Spurn lifeboat was warned by members of a life-saving crew who had been out all night on rough weather watch and immediately raced to the *Deveron*'s assistance.

Heavy seas, however, prevented the lifeboat crew getting alongside the *Deveron*. As the tide fell the trawler was left high and dry and a Withernsea doctor walked over the sands and boarded the vessel. He found the third hand, Mr William Belt, seriously injured.

Tragically, Mr Belt, who had taken the trip as a favour to the company, died later in Hull Royal Infirmary from his injuries. He had been sailing from Grimsby for 30 years although this was his first North Sea trip for two years. Mr Belt had fished from Grimsby during the war and in 1944 had been awarded the MBE for his skill in navigating an open boat into a Faroese port after his ship had been mined.

Line Aboard

In heavy weather he had taken over the boat and succeeded in making port after 36 hours. Shortly after the grounding of the *Deveron* the weather started deteriorating rapidly but a life-saving team managed to get a line aboard the trawler. Plans were laid to get a tug, which was standing by, to tow her safely off. The problem would be whether or not the vessel could get close enough to allow the manoeuvre to take place.

Rescue squads were on hand to help the crew in any new emergency. Only 50 yards of water had separated the *Deveron* from the watchers who had gathered on the shore, but the seas were running so high that it was impossible to attempt to get to her by boat. The roar of the fierce gale prevented shouted messages being heard and semaphore signals were used by the men aboard the stricken trawler to send out an SOS for a doctor. All members of the crew, except the injured man, were safe and remained on board.

The plight of the *Deveron* had been first noticed as dawn broke that January day. A team of life-savers, under their leader, Mr J Clubley were patrolling the spit of land which curved round to Spurn Point some four miles south of the spot. In a heavy gale the lifeboat alerted by Mr Clubley, put out to sea, but found it too dangerous to attempt to manoeuvre close enough to the

84. The Deveron left high and dry at Spurn.

Deveron to take the injured man off.

The *Deveron* had sailed for the North Sea fishing grounds only a few days earlier. She was under the command of Skipper G J Horner, of Huddlestone Road, Grimsby who was making his first trip in her. As night fell, efforts to get the trawler off the beach got underway — but unsuccessfully. Plans were laid to get another tug, of lighter draught, to the scene for a new attempt the following night.

A Week's Wait

But an owners' representative warned: "If the tug is unsuccessful tonight because of low tides then we may have to wait a week or so for the higher tides before other attempts are made."

How right he was to prove to be.

It was 12 days before the vessel was finally pulled clear by the tug *Barnham* which towed the trawler into Grimsby Fish Docks. The story of the vicar and the trawler was related by both Grimsby freelance journalist Mr Charles Ekberg and Mr Bill Taylor, formerly of The UK Trawlers Mutual Insurance Co Ltd.

Mr Taylor, who went out to inspect the trawler and to help with the rescue, said the trawler had been coming into port to land the third hand when she went aground. He went aboard the vessel and tried to fire a rocket line to the lifeboat crew.

"I tried three times. When I pulled it the fourth time it went like a rocket and nearly took the head off the coxswain," Mr Taylor said.

The *Deveron* was 44-years-old when she went aground. She had been built in 1905 by Earle's Shipbuilding and Engineering of Hull for D Line Steam Fishing Company of Grimsby. She moved to new owners, W Garetts, in 1929 and then to C Dobson of Grimsby in 1938. She later saw service with the Perihelion Steam Fishing Co and after the war went to the Deveron Steam Fishing Co (Butts).

One man with striking memories of her was Mr Fred Lee, of Runswick Court, Grimsby.

He remembered sailing on her as a deckie along with Les White and Dick Wignall on a trip to Iceland.

"The skipper was a Yorkie, George Davis. We sailed with the port and starboard sides full of coal, in a gale of wind. By the time we got to Flamborough we had lost the port side coal, said Mr Lee.

The trawler carried that weather to the Faroes where the vessel anchored.

"We eventually left the Faroes in a northerly gale to dodge across to Iceland. The next day I went on watch with two other deckies to find the bridge windows put in by the weather. We had to steer with our frocks on," recalled Mr Lee.

There were also technical problems with the compass — and the skipper put that right by pouring three bottles of whisky in. Mr Lee went below only to find the trawler leaking like a sieve.

"We could do nothing because of the weather. We finally arrived at Grimms Isle on the north side of Iceland where we finally got our gear shot after 10 days steaming down there.

Worst Day

"That was the worst day's work I had ever done when I signed on that ship," said Mr Lee.

The *Deveron*'s last duty was to help a steamer which had turned on it side in severe gales early in 1953.

The *Hebble* was lying on its side in Humber Graving Dock at Immingham. A plan to raise her was drawn up with the idea of having a dress rehearsal one day and the operation the next. However, the dress rehearsal became the real thing. Two large railway engines pulled heavy steel hawsers through a series of pulleys while the *Deveron*, loaded with ballast, acted as an anchor in an adjacent lockpit. The operation worked and the *Hebble* came upright as the dock was filled with water.

Just a few days later the *Deveron* was towed into Grimsby where her gravel ballast was discharged and she was scrapped.

The Ross Revenge

From the record breaker to record player — that's the story of the Grimsby trawler *Ross Revenge*. For this German-built vessel, which notched up an amazing number of records during her fishing career, was to become the radio station Radio Caroline. With the highest floating radio mast ever erected, the trawler set about bunting a new catch — listeners. It was all a far cry from the days of the vessel that caught everyone's attention with her marvellously successful trips to the distant water grounds. But the *Ross Revenge* was not actually built for Grimsby owners. She was ordered by Isbjorninn, an Icelandic company which, incidentally, opened one of the most modern fish processing plants in the word a couple of years ago.

Built in Bremerhaven in 1960, the 978-ton trawler was one of a series of four produced for the company. She was originally skippered by Asgeir Gislason who was to become a regular visitor to the port of Grimsby. After only some 18 months fishing for the Icelandic industry the trawler was sold to Ross Trawlers Ltd, of Grimsby.

Change of Name

And in the words of one fisherman: "That's when she began to earn a fortune."

It was on 29 August 1963, that the *Evening Telegraph* carried the news of the vessel's move to Grimsby where her name was to be changed from the *Freyr* to the *Ross Revenge*. A conventional trawler, she was fitted for fishing on either side and was to become the largest sidewinder operating from the UK. She was 210ft between perpendiculars with a moulded beam of 33ft 9in and a depth of 18ft.

This was bigger than the previous conventional trawler, the *Cape Oranto* of Hull, which was 194ft between perpendiculars with a gross tonnage of 823. A crew under the command of Skipper J N Kerr left Grimsby for Reykjavik to bring the trawler to Grimsby. Skipper Kerr had previously been in charge of the *Ross Renown*. The *Ross Revenge* was powered by a 2,300hp Workspoor diesel engine, driving a variable pitch propeller which gave a trial speed of 16 knots. The fish rooms were exceptionally large, totalling 27,000 cubic feet.

She was soon into the swing of fishing from the port and making big money. Then on 24 February 1970 Skipper Jim Meadows became the toast of his crew when he set up a new Grimsby port record for the second time in four weeks. The *Ross Revenge* hauled in £20,621 after a 25-day trip to the Norway Coast — smashing all previous records by Grimsby vessels.

By now Ross Trawlers had been taken over by British United Trawlers and the *Ross Revenge* brought them 2,977 kits back including 1,250 kits of haddock. The catch was so big that it took two days to land it.

The previous month Skipper Meadows made £19,003 on the *Velinda* but that one was beaten a few days later by the *William Wilberforce*.

Of his record-breaking *Ross Revenge* trip he said at the time: "It was the haddock which made the trip. We had quite a bit of luck finding it in bunches, which is not usual with spawning haddock." Sixteen months later he took the *Ross Revenge* out again and came back to smash the British Trawler earnings record. The sale amassed £28,375 — incredible for the time.

The *Ross Revenge* brought home an impressive 3,683 kits. Ironically it came from the north-west cape of Iceland, a ground eventually closed to Grimsby vessels by the Icelandic 50-mile fishing limit. And the daily earnings

85. The Ross Revenge in her new role as Radio Caroline.

of £1,418 was also a record. It was all the more remarkable because the trip had been made in mid-summer — a time when fish was often left unsold on the Grimsby fish market. In the first six months of that year the *Ross Revenge* had earned a healthy £121,000.

The previous British record was held by the *Ross Renown* which made just under £28,000 in January. The spate of high prices on the market that day also brought bonuses for other vessels. The *Boston Concord* grossed £15,266 from a distant water trip while, from the Westerly grounds, the *Ross Cheetah* made £12,225 and the *Ross Genet* £11,354. For the *Ross Revenge* the records continued to fall.

On 29 September 1973, again under the command of Skipper Meadows, she sailed home to yet another port record grossing of £38,253.

Fall in Prices

A drop in the level of fish prices meant that she only grossed £44,697 — well below the port and world record. Skipper Meadows was in command again. A Fisheries Ministry spokesman said:

"If only the catch had been made two months ago it would have shattered all previous records and probably topped the £70,000 mark." Because of the fall in prices cod was only fetching around £18 a kit. And in the middle of the 1970s the troubles which were to eventually spell the end of the fishing career of the *Ross Revenge* began to have their effect.

She landed another bumper catch on 14 April 1975, some 3,196 kits making £54,493. But a spokesman for BUT pointed out it was rather a "flukey" result with the price of the catch being inflated by the dearth of fish caused by the problems within the industry.

86. Grimsby trawler the Ross Revenge.

Four months later, on 26 August she got the best return by a vessel for some time — grossing £44,567 for her 2,706 kits. The trawler had been on a 26-day trip to Iceland and returned with a large amount of cod.

Skipper Meadows was again in charge.

Things continued to improve and on 13 July 1976, the *Ross Revenge* again returned from Iceland with the best trip for months. She made £57,344 for her 2,558 kits of mainly cod.

And this time she had done it not under Skipper Meadows but under the command of Skipper Ray Pepper of Hull.

But Grimsby's record-breaking man was not to be away from the scene for long.

And towards the end of August that year he combined his talents with the catching power of the *Ross Revenge* to achieve that one title which had evaded him — the world earnings record.

A Proud Return

The trawler proudly brought home 3,000 kits of Icelandic cod and grossed a massive £75,597. It was the second outstanding trip in a week. The *Ross Ramillies* had earlier set a new port record at £64,000. A Hull-based trawler, the *Hammond Innes*, had set the previous world record at £73,000 some 18 months earlier. Skipper Meadows admitted he had felt "a little wobbly" when he realised just what the trip had made. Trawlers had started returning with big catches after the pack ice had opened up and created several lakes where huge stocks of fish had begun to congregate.

But Skipper Meadows stressed that the ice had since closed again, covering the best grounds.

Despite the achievement the celebrations were tempered with caution in the Fish Docks. The owners pointed out that the success did not detract in any way from the very serious problems facing the fishing industry. Those problems were finally to catch up with the *Ross Revenge*. Reduced fishing opportunity and the high cost of sending such a large vessel to the distant water grounds made her uneconomical to run.

On 17 August 1979, the *Evening Telegraph* carried the news that she had been sold. But luckily she was not going to the scrapyard. Instead she went to be converted for a new role as a North Sea wreck recovery vessel.

Four years later, she was bright red with a new name, Imagine, having been bought by Radio Caroline's founder with United States backing.

The Ross Hawk

The Grimsby trawler *Ross Hawk* became something of a tourist attraction 15 years ago when she ran aground close to Cleethorpes Pier. For days, as efforts to free her went on, she attracted crowds of sightseers and even had parties of school-children drawing her! The drama began on the day of 6 March 1968 as 80-knot gales lashed the harbour. Heavy snow was falling as conditions drove the trawler on to the beach and within sight of one of the crew's homes. Coastguards from Donna Nook raced to the scene and fired rocket and breeches launchers on the pier. Police and ambulance crews stood by on the shore in case they were needed.

The *Ross Hawk* stayed put all night with her 12-man crew still aboard. The powerful tug *Lady Alma* made the short trip to the scene armed with rockets and lines.

Strong winds continued to batter the *Ross Hawk* and she was pushed further and further ashore. At first light the tug made a bid to get the trawler off but was unable to get anywhere near the ship.

When the high tide arrived there was only 5ft of water around the trawler which was just 150 yards off the pier.

Flat on the Sand

And Mr Ken Blessed who acted as a spokesman for J H Piggott's, the tug's owners, told a reporter: "Tides will be falling all the time now up till Sunday. It is unlikely we shall be able to refloat her before then.

"The ship is flat on the sand and there is no danger of her keeling over. Because the weather is abating I don't think she will move up much further. There is no danger to the pier."

The *Lady Alma* was commanded by Skipper Peter Gibney who had helped refloat another Grimsby trawler, the *Ross Genet*, which ran ashore in January that year. During the night the tug had managed to get a line aboard the *Ross Hawk* but this had parted with the gale force winds. The tug was unable to get any closer because of the danger of running aground herself.

Skipper of the *Ross Hawk* was Bob Sinclair who telephoned his wife that night to let her know that the crew were OK. Meanwhile plans were being laid to get off the 250 kits of valuable fish the trawler was carrying.

"Operation Fishlift" was put into action.

A fleet of lorries made their way to the beach to take away the fish to the market. Between 5 pm and 8 pm on 7 March the work went ahead. The trawler crew and about 15 other workers were engaged in the operation. Two chutes were thrown over the side of the vessel and fish was shovelled down into waiting kit baskets on a trailer.

A tractor provided a shuttle service between the ship and the promenade

87. The Ross Hawk pictured in Grimsby in 1961. She was one of the last big trawlers to fish out of the port.

where the baskets were loaded on to lorries. After about an hour's work it was estimated that more than 100 kits — or 1,000 stones — of fish had been removed ready for the following day

. Whilst the crew worked feverishly to beat both the incoming tide and the fading light, an excavator and bulldozers were digging out a deep trench behind the *Ross Hawk*. It was hoped that the midnight high tide might refloat the vessel but she was still firmly aground the next day. Although it was bitterly cold many people crowded on the beach to see the trawler and the fish unloading operation.

They were able to get up close to the trawler until the tide turned when they were advised by police to get to dry ground. Among those sightseers were relatives of the crew.

The third hand, Mr Thomas McArthur, got quite a reception. On the beach waiting to greet him were his wife, daughter and grandchildren. He told them that the previous night had been bad but that he and his colleagues had been all right.

He told how the anchor chain had parted while the trawler had been in the shipping channel and how a call for assistance had gone out.

He said at the time: "We must have fired about three rockets at the *Lady Alma* and they the same at us, but they all missed."

For days afterwards unsuitable tides were to thwart the efforts to refloat the trawlers. But on the night of 15 March 1968 she was successfully refloated. The tug *Lady Elsie* pulled her off the sand at about 6 pm and an hour later she was back in Grimsby Fish Docks. This time there had been little difficulty in pulling her off and she had suffered only minor damage despite her long spell on the beach. The *Ross Hawk* was only eight years old when she grounded.

She was the second of a group of six diesel-engined vessels built for Ross Trawlers of Grimsby and was launched at the Selby shipyard of Cochrane and Sons Ltd. The launching and naming ceremony was performed by Mrs Appleyard, wife of Mr W P Appleyard, a director of Ross Group.

For Skipper Jack Ibbotson it was a change from the old to the new when he took the trawler because for the previous three years he had been in command of one of the port's old stagers, the *Restrivo*, which was then 47 years old. He was reported to be highly delighted with his new command The *Ross Hawk* was to land her last trip in Grimsby in November 1971. Ross had by then become a part of the British United Trawlers operation and the 107ft vessel was transferred to Fleetwood. She did not stay there long before moving to Aberdeen. Eventually the trawler was converted to oil rig standby work.

She transferred to Lowestoft to undertake similar work.

88. *The memorial in Grimsby's Fishing Chapel.*

The End of an Era

It is hard to comprehend today, but in 1929 there were well over 1,000 trawlers registered as sailing from Grimsby.

Just imagine it . . . a thousand or more ships, each providing regular work for a dozen or more men at sea and even more ashore . . . a dock teeming with vessels, so many that it was claimed you could walk from one side of the dock to another without ever getting your feet wet.

There were the Iceland ships, the Faroes trawlers, the North Seas, the snibbies, a list which stretched from GY 1 right up to GY 1355.

This is the list in full with names of owners in most cases.

Gy 1 **Emu**, *Taylors; Gy 2* **Ravenna**, *Trawlers WS and Gy; Gy 3* **Rajah**, *Sleights; Gy 4* **Hermona**, *Peterson; Gy 5* **Andes**, *Bannister; Gy 6* **Algoma**, *Bannister; Gy 7* **Midnight Son**, *Grimsby Seine Fishing Co; Gy 8* **Gleaning,** *Cox; Gy 10* **Lord Cromer**, *Flotsam SFC; Gy 14* **Rivière**, *Earl SFC; Gy 15* **Maelstrom**, *Grimsby Seine Fishing Co; Gy 19* **Chimaera**, *Franklins; Gy 20* **Leonora**, *Lindsey; Gy 22* **Roto**, *Sleights; Gy 23* **Renovo**, *Sleights; Gy 24* **Lapwing**, *Lindsey; Gy 27* **Herring Queen**, *Atmosphere SFC; Gy 28* **Thealby,** *Atmosphere SFC; Gy 30* **Reliance**, *Croft Baker; Gy 32* **Ingomar**, *Bacons; Gy 33* **Ethel**, *Chidwick; Gy 34* **JS**, *Premier; Gy 35* **Broican**, *Croft Baker; Gy 36* **Leo**, *Lindsey; Gy 37* **Kingsway**, *Strand SFC; Gy 38* **Kennymore**, *Baskcomb; Gy 39* **Gurth**, *United; Gy 41* **Silverna**, *Peterson; Gy 42* **EES**, *Premier; Gy 45* **Atmosphere**, *Garratt and Jeffs; Gy 46* **Carency**, *Earl SFC; Gy 47* **Anson**, *Dobsons; Gy 48* **Earl Essex**, *Strand; Gy 51* **Cineraria**, *Grimsby Seiners; Gy 52* **Buffalo**, *Garratt and Jeffs; Gy 54* **Vidette**, *TWS and Gy; Gy 55* **Salacon**, *Standard; Gy 56* **Barbuda**, *Grant and Baker; Gy 57* **Vesta**, *TWS and Gy; Gy 59* **Sandringham**, *Queen SFC; Gy 60* **Tiger's Eye**, *William Allen; Gy 64* **Janus II**, *Baskcomb; Gy 66* **Venture**, *Bacons; Gy 67* **Viola**, *Arctic SFC; Gy 70* **Sabvini**, *Earl SFC; Gy 71* **Barbados**, *Grant and Baker; Gy 72* **Manx Hero**, *Beeley and Sleight; Gy 73* **Warstar**, *Earl SFC; Gy 74* **Orpheus**, *Arctic; Gy 76* **Aquarius**, *Lindsey; Gy 77* **William Wesney**, *Crampins; Gy 78* **Barle**, *St Malo SFC; Gy 79* **Courser**, *Dobsons; Gy 84* **Nebris**, *Consols; Gy 86* **Senga**, *Osbornes; Gy 87* **Onward**, *Forward SFC; Gy 88* **White Knight**, *Grimsby Seiners; Gy 90* **Holyrood**, *Queens; Gy 91* **Pelican**, *Sleights; Gy 92* **Treasure**, *Whites; Gy 94* **Meror**, *TWS and Gy; Gy 96* **Deveron**, *Garrett and Jeffs; Gy 98* **Forward II**, *Baskcomb; Gy 101* **Ebor Bell**, *Chapmans; Gy 103* **Bengal**, *Grant and Baker; Gy 105* **Boy Germyn**, *AVPF; Gy 108* **Itonian**, *Consols; Gy 110* **Northward**, *Forwards; Gy 112* **Abronia**, *Baskcombs; Gy 113* **Bromelia**, *Baskcombs; Gy 116* **Lord Darling**, *Consols; Gy 117* **Aucuba**, *Grant and Robinson; Gy 121* **Lilias**, *McD Scott; Gy 122* **Koorah**, *Cox and Cox; Gy 130* **Essex**, *Dobsons; Gy 131* **Soranus**, *Rushworth; Gy 132* **Wallena**, *Bacons; Gy 135* **Rononia**, *Bacons; Gy 136* **Edith Constance**, *Bishops; Gy 137* **Flotsam**, *Flotsam SFC; Gy 138* **Silvernight**, *Grimsby Seiners; Gy 139* **Zonia**, *Baskcombs; Gy 140* **Fortuna**, *Sleights; Gy 141* **Greynight**, *Grimsby Seiners; Gy 143* **Agami**, *Grimsby Trawler Owners; Gy 144* **Ottilie**, *TWS and Gy; Gy 148* **Yucatan**, *Chapmans; Gy 149* **Donalda**, *Hill; Gy 150* **Exyahne**, *Croft Baker; Gy 154* **Dalby**, *Dalby SFC; Gy 157* **Tokio II**, *Diamond; Gy 159* **Liberia**, *Lindsey; Gy 162* **Ormonde**, *Arctic; Gy 163* **Sicyon**, *Standard; Gy 167* **Kimberley**, *Diamond; Gy 169* **Fisherman,** *Sir Ernest Sleight; Gy 171* **Ophir II**, *Forward; Gy 172* **Aurora**, *Dobson; Gy 173* **Ariadne**, *Dobsons; Gy 174* **Sialkot**, *Palestine SFC; Gy 175* **Samurai**, *Sleights; Gy 179* **Shikari**, *Staples; Gy 181* **Riano**, *Sleights; Gy 183* **Ladysmith**, *Diamond; Gy 184* **Georgette**, *Consols; Gy 185* **Rigoletto**, *Sleights; Gy 186* **Shade**, *Grimsby Seiners; Gy 187* **Cloudarch**, *Grimsby Seiners; Gy 188* **Blacknight**, *Grimsby Seiners; Gy 189 Grimsby Seiners; Gy 190* **Merlin**, *Orontes SFC;*

Gy 191 **Darogh**, Bowerings; Gy 192 **Russell**, Grants; Gy 193 **Roaming**, Coppin; Gy 195 **Rodney**, Dobson; Gy 197 **Perihelion**, Dryburgh; Gy 200 **Ostero**, Garratt and Jeffs; Gy 201 **Dragon**, Allens; Gy 202 **Waldorf**, Butts; Gy 209 **Empyrean**, Lindsey; Gy 211 **Virginian**, Onwards; Gy 213 **Ontario**, Dominion SFC; Gy 214 **Campina**, Crampins; Gy 215 **Quail**, Baskcomb; Gy 220 **Annie**, Kings; Gy 221 **Cadella**, Crampins; Gy 223 **Dahlia**, Baskcomb; Gy 225 **William Ashton**, Crampins; Gy 228 **Thomas Threasher**, Grimsby SFC; Gy 229 **Relonzo**, Sleights; Gy 230 **Sheraton**, Standard; Gy 231 **Joseph Annison**, Perihelion; Gy 233 **Erillus**, Consols; Gy 235 **Volante**, Dobsons; Gy 237 **Lord Shaftesbury**, Consols; Gy 239 **Amorelle**, Consols; Gy 243 **Emilion**, Consols; Gy 247 **Bombay**, Grant and Bakers; Gy 250 **Bertha**, Gough; Gy 252 **Evlyn**, Lambert; Gy 253 **Retako**, Sleights; Gy 254 **Sapphire**, Perihelion; Gy 257 **Vidonia**, Arctic; Gy 258 **Runnymede**, Chapmans; Gy 259 **Myrtle Spring**, Flotsam; Gy 264 **Returno**, Sleights; Gy 265 **Restrivo**, Sleights; Gy 267 **Endeavor**, Croft; Gy 268 **Carmania II**, Strand; Gy 270 **River Tummell**, Consols; Gy 272 **River Kelvin**, Consols; Gy 273 **River Garry**, Consols; Gy 274 **Congo**, Trawlers WS and Gy; Gy 276 **River Findhorn**, Consols; Gy 277 **River Don**, Consols; Gy 278 **River Ayr**, Consols; Gy 279 **River Lossie**, Consols; Gy 280 **Kirby**, Consols; Gy 282 **Ladas**, Baskcombs; Gy 283 **Witham**, Consols; Gy **Electric**, Munning; Gy 287 **Helping**, Copping; Gy 289 **River Nith**, Consols; Gy 292 **Hortensia**, Garratt and Jeffs; Gy 293 **River Leven**, Cosols; Gy 294 **Abelia**, Baskcomb; Gy 295 **Sanson**, Standard; Gy 298 **Reperio**, Sleights; Gy 299 **Telia**, Baskcomb; Gy 300 **Morvino**, Bacon; Gy 302 **Wistaria**, Baskcomb; Gy 304, **Raymont**, TWS and Gy; Gy 305 **Louis Botha**, Earl; Gy 306 **Marlborough**, Queen; Gy 307 **Destin**, Earl; Gy 310 **Douro**, Trawlers WS and Gy; Gy 313 **Rayallieu**, Overseas SFC; Gy 314 **James and Susan**, Chidwick; Gy 315 **Frascati**, Strand; Gy 318 **Claire**, Grant; Gy 320 **Roxano**, Sleights; Gy 232 **Grenada**, Grant and Baker; Gy 325 **George Aunger**, Bunch; Gy 327 **Julia Wood**, Harper; Gy 333 **Othello**, Forward; Gy 334 **James Evans**, Taylors; Gy 336 **Bellona**, Consols; Gy 340 **Avon**, St Malo SFC; Gy 340 **War Lord**, Harrison; Gy 344 **Dentaria**, Baskcomb; Gy 346 **Epinard**, Rushworth; Gy 348 **Youlan**, Baskcomb; Gy 349 **Bloom** Garratt and Jeffs; Gy 350 **Staunton**, Standard; Gy 351 **Floreat**, Beeley; Gy 354 **Peken**, Diamond; Gy 356 **Orizaba**, Forward; Gy 357 **Athenian**, Onward; Gy 359 **Ashby**, Dutton; Gy 361 **Noveli**, Bacon; Gy 363 **Nylghua**, Garratt; Gy 364 **Chikara**, Garratt, Gy 366 **Berenga**, Trawlers WS and Gy; Gy 370 **Melba**, Chapmans; Gy 373 **Revello**, Sleights; Gy 379 **Garnet**, Perihelion; Gy 380 **Reporto**, Sleights; Gy 381 **Kuvera**, Consols; Gy 382 **Genhara**, F. Sleights; Gy 383 **Jacinth**, Bunsh; Gy 384 **Triton**, Garratt and Jeffs; Gy 386 **Weymouth**, Garratt and Jeffs; Gy 387 **Manx King**, Earl; Gy 388 **Clifton**, Moss; Gy 389 **Taipoo**, Diamond; Gy 390 **Somersby**, Bostons; Gy 391 **Jonquil**, Baskcomb; Gy 392 **Cynthia**, TWS and Gy; Gy 393 **Malaga**, Bostons; Gy 394 **Hekla**, Oleson and Ogmundsson; Gy 395 **Lord Shrewsbury**, Trawlers WS and Gy; Gy 399 **Prospect**, Hardy; Gy 400 **Spurn Head**, John Robinson; Gy 401 **Lynx II**, Thos. Robinson; Gy 402 **Gardenia**, Baskcomb; Gy 403 **Tidal Range**, Selby Lowndes; Gy 405 **Jaboo II**, Baskcomb and Northcote; Gy 408 **Gloria**, Overseas; Gy 410 **Belover**, Garratt; Gy 411 **Orontes**, Orontes SFC; Gy 412 **Ocean Victor**, Garratt; Gy 414 **Gloria II**, Jack Croft; Gy 417 **Ocean Fisher**, Garratt; Gy 418 **Triumph**, Parrott; Gy 420 **Cedric**, United; Gy 424 **Cedric**, United; Gy 424 **Seven**, Hardy; Gy 425 **Arthur H. Johnson**, Roninson; Gy 430 **Median**, Onward; Gy 431 **The Throne**, Robinson; Gy 434 **Tyrwhitt**, Orontes; Gy 433 **Green Howard**, Consols; Gy 434 **Gunner**, Green Howard; Gy 435 **Belvoir Castle**, Crampin; Gy 436 **Cuirass**, Crown; Gy 437 **Romily**, Bacon; Gy 338 **Dagon**, Consols; Gy 440 **Santora**, Premier; Gy 441 **Ivy West**, Craske; Gy 443 **The Lily**, Spensley and Kent; Gy 444 **Fezenta**, Strand; Gy 445 **St Keverne**, Gy 446 **Earl Warwick**, Bunch; Gy 447 **Drummer Boy**, Thos Robinson; Gy 449 **Earl Grannard**, Harold Bacon; Gy 451 **Bluebird Anderson** and Taylor; Gy 452 **Samaritan**, Baker; Gy 456 **Alaburn**, Premier; Gy 457 **Irene**, Sam Chapman; Gy 458 **St Minver**, Bunsh; Gy 461 **Juliana**, Perihelion; Gy 462 **Lord Birkenhead**, Crampin; Gy 463 **Lord Talbot**, Perihelion; Gy 464 **Betty Mork**, Oleson; Gy 465 **Guyne Thorne**, Rushworth; Gy 466 **Vendora Atlas**; Gy 468 **Washington, Harley**; Gy 469 **Embassy**, Grant; Gy 470 **Thankful**, Jordison; Gy 472 **Caribrooke**, Queen; Gy 473 **Lysander**, Baskcomb; Gy 474 **King Erik**, Baskcomb; Gy 478 **Lombard**,

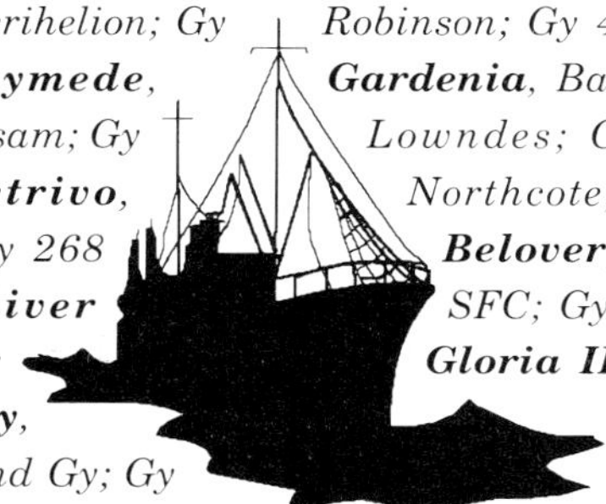

Lindsey; Gy 479 **King Harald**, *Baskcomb; Gy 482* **Magnolia**, *Baskcomb; Gy 483* **Veresis**, *Atlas; Gy 484* **Minoru**, *Baskcomb; Gy 485* **Gadra**, *Grant and Baker; Gy 489* **Providence**,*,West; Gy 490* **George and Francis**, *Gillard; Gy 496* **Stalker**, *Lindsey; Gy 498* **Consort**, *Queen; Gy 504* **Seriema**, *Baskcomb; Gy 506* **Worsley**, *Dale; Gy 507* **Recordo**, *Sleight; Gy 509* **Lord Selbourne**, *Earl; Gy 511* **Varanis**, *Arctic; Gy 512* **Recondo**, *Sleights, Gy 516* **War Grey**, *Cox and Cox; Gy 523* **St Malo**, *St Malo SFC; Gy 536 Huxley, Jeffries; Gy 542* **Manx Princess**, *Bowering; Gy 546* **Stromo**, *Orontes; Gy 557* **China**, *Baskcomb; Gy 558* **Saltaire**, *Thos Robinson; Gy 563* **Lord Beaconsfield**, *Consols; Gy 569* **Prince Victor**, *Trawlers WS and Gy; Gy 570* **India**, *Baskcomb; Gy 581* **Edward VII**, *Sleights; Gy 588* **Alberia**, *Crown; Gy 593* **Exceed II**, *King; Gy 594* **Riby**, *Grant; Gy 597* **Napier**, *Forward; Gy 598* **Flandre**, *Earl; Gy 603* **Diamond**, *Moss; Gy 605* **Ronso**, *Sleights; Gy 608* **The Tower**, *Tower SFC; Gy 611* **Beru**, *Grant; Gy 612* **Durga**, *Sleights; Gy 613* **Emerald**, *Moss; Gy 615* **Victory**, *Bilton; Gy 617* **Premier**, *Chapman; Gy 618* **Clara**, *Crawford; Gy 623* **Regardo**, *Sleights; Gy 625* **Reconso**, *Sleights; Gy 629* **Premier II**, *Bilton; Gy 630* **Nairana**, *TWS and Gy; Gy 631* **Escallonia**, *Baskcomb; Gy 634* **Casssoaway**, *Baskcomb; Gy 641* **Lacerta**, *Lindsey; Gy 642* **Croxby**, *Grant; Gy 644* **Garu**, *Grant and Baker; Gy 645* **Cayrian**, *Trawlers Ws and Gy; Gy 646* **Partian**, *Onward; Gy 648* **Athelstan**, *Thos Robinson; Gy 650* **Houbra**, *Baskcomb; Gy 654* **Reformo**, *Sleights; Gy 663, Ralco Sleights; Gy 665* **Manx Admiral**, *Sleights; Gy 676* **Star of the South**, *Jeanne Nierinck; Gy 679* **Garola**, *Grant and Baker; Gy 680* **Quercia**, *Great Grimsby and East Coast; Gy 683* **Night Rider**, *Nocturne; Gy 687* **Libra**, *Trawlers WS and Gy; Gy 690* **Flying Wing**, *Thos Robinson; Gy 695* **Pola**, *Sharp; Gy 696* **Sheldon**, *Standard; Gy 698* **Hilaria**, *Paynes; Gy 700* **Lovania**, *Earl; Gy 701* **Hondo**, *Diamond; Gy 704* **Edwardian**, *Gy 707* **Raetia**, *Grimsby and East Coast; Gy* **Blanche**, *Chidwick; Gy 712* **Fort William**, *Irvin; Gy 714* **Solon**, *Standard; Gy 716* **Pavlova**, *Baskcomb; Gy 717* **Conisboro Castle**, *Nielsen; Gy 721* **Remexo**, *Sleights; Gy 723* **Tartan**, *Thos Robinson; Gy 725* **Kalso**, *Bannister; Gy 728* **Iranian**, *Thos Robinson; Gy 733* **Great Admiral**, *Baskcomb; Gy 737* **Prefect**, *Atlas; Gy 739* **G. E. Foster**, *Canadian Fish and Cold Storage; Gy 744* **Tagalia**, *Overseas; Gy 745* **Chrysa**, *Staples; Gy 755* **Caspian**, *Trawlers WS and Gy; Gy 758* **Imperia**, *Trawlers WS and Gy; Gy 759* **Lord Northcliffe**, *Trawlers WS and Gy; Gy 762* **James Carruthers**, *Canadian Fish and Cold Storage; Gy 768* **Lord Cecil**, *Trawlers Ws and Gy; Gy 771* **MacDuff**,*, Melhuish; Gy 782* **Unexpected, Kirman**; *Gy 784* **Helios**, *Thos Robinson; Gy 788* **Desiree**, *Trawlers Ws and Gy; Gy 792* **Caulonia**, *Strand; Gy 795* **Angolian**, *Onward; Gy 800* **Emmanual**, *Harper; Gy 801* **Siluria**, *Gy 802* **Ann Lewis**, *Stookes; Gy 804* **Fentonian**, *Thos Robinson; Gy 809* **Silica**, *Great Grimsby and East Coast; Gy 810* **Strephon**, *Standard; Gy 811* **Hercules II**, *Trawlers WS and Gy; Gy 819* **Warland**, *Earl; Gy 822* **Night Hawk**, *Grimsby SFC; Gy 825* **Buzzard**, *Bannisters; Gy 826* **Renzo**, *Sleights; Gy 827* **Vanator**, *Garratt and Jeffs; Gy 828* **Portia**, *A. Black; Gy 829* **Rehearo**, *Sleights; Gy 830* **Calverton**, *Moss; Gy 835* **Rock of Ages**, *Stratton; Gy 836* **Rodino**, *Sleights; Gy 839* **Rodosto**, *Sleights; Gy 841* **PAT**, *Townsend; Gy 843* **Remagio**, *Sleights; Gy 844* **Dorando**, *Trawlers WS and Gy; Gy 846* **Pride**, *Chapman; Gy 848* **Trojan**, *Chant; Gy 849* **Sea Gull**, *Croft; Gy 851* **Remillo**, *Sleights; Gy 853* **Sweeper**, *Baskcomb; Gy 856* **St Cloud**, *Pattison; Gy 857* **War Wing**, *Baskcomb; Gy 858* **Sargon**, *Standard; Gy 862* **Cortina**, *Trawlers WS and Gy; Gy 866* **Glatian**, *Thos Robinson; Gy 876* **Storm Centre**, *Jeffs and Garratt; Gy 879* **Lord Durham**, *Consols; Gy 885* **Valmont**, *Victoria; Gy 886* **Violet**, *Parrott; Gy 887* **Joseph Burgin**, *Grimsby SFC; Gy 891* **Lord Allendale**, *Consols; Gy 894* **Rinovia**, *Little; Gy 898* **Lord Percy**, *Consols; Gy 901* **Saurian**, *Croft Baker; Gy 907* **Thunderstone**, *Earl; Gy 908* **Carieda**, *Bacons; Gy 909* **Lord Ashby**, *Consols; Gy 914* **Riskato**, *Sleights; Gy 915* **Valeska**, *Earls; Gy 916* **Lord Wimborne**, *Consols; Gy 918* **Cancer**, *Lindsey; Gy 920* **Prince Leo**, *Trawlers WS and Gy; Gy 923* **Wimpole**, *Rushworth; Gy 924* **Unitia**, *Grimsby and East Coast; Gy 926* **Resparko**, *Sleights: Gy 928* **Sethon**, *Standard; Gy 929* **Swanland Hall**, *Collins; Gy 930* **Wyndham**, *Consols; Gy 932* **Sabreur**, *Strand; Gy 933* **Ross Castle**, *Champlin; Gy 935* **Scarron**, *Standard; Gy 938* **Lybian Onward**; *Gy 939* **Etruscan**, *Thos Robinson; Gy 941* **Royalo**, *Sleights; Gy 942* **Resolvo**, *Sleights; Gy 944* **Deanside**, *Baskcomb; Gy 945* **The Tetrach**, *Baskcomb; Gy 946* **Ristango**, *Sleights; Gy*

948 **Oakwold**, H.W. Chant; Gy 949 **Ampula**, Loyal Steam Fishing; Gy 951 **Retrudo**, Sleights; Gy 954 **Vindelecia**, Great Grimsby and East Coast; Gy 958 **Delphine**, Consols; Gy 959 **Chancellor**, Sam Chapman Jnr; Gy 960 **Simerson**, Standard; Gy 963 **Castor**, Lindsey; Gy 969 **Elmira**, Consols; Gy **Eynside**, Baskcomb; Gy 975 **Offa**, Consols; Gy 976 **Saturn**, Trawlers WS and Gy; Gy 980 **Lapageria**, Robinsons; Gy 981 **Delphinus**, Trawler WS and Gy; Gy 982 **Quixotic**, Grimsby Steam Fishing; Gy 983 **Frank**, A.King; Gy 984 **Sarpedon**, Standard Steam Fishing; Gy 985 **Jeria**, Great Grimsby and East Coast; Gy 994 **Rugby**, A. Grant; Gy 998 **Windsor**, Queen; Gy 999 **Linnet**, Overseas Steam Fishing; Gy 1001 **Balmoral**, Queen; Gy 1003 **Robina**, Trawlers WS and Gy; Gy 1004 **Argo**, J. Snowdon; Gy 1012 **Susarian**, Standard; Gy 1017 **Castorial**, Great Grimsby and East Coast; Gy 1018 **Moravia**, Great Grimsby and East Coast; Gy 1019 **Respondo**, Sleights; Gy 1021 **Corcyra**, Earl Steam Fishing; Gy 1022 **Capricornus**, TrawlersWS and Gy; Gy 1023 **Leys**, Queen; Gy 1024 **Simpson**, Standard; Gy 1025 **General Botha**, John Lewis; Gy 1026 **Helvetia**, Great Grimsby and East Coast; Gy 1029 **Resmilo**, Sleights; Gy 1037 **War Duke**, Bacons; Gy 1038 **Fifnella**, Consols; Gy 1039 **Favorita**, Consols; Gy 1040 **Fiat**, Consols; Gy 1041 **Franc Tireur**, Consols; Gy 1042 **Floria**, Consols; Gy 1043 **Honoria**, S. Bunch; Gy 1045 **Pioneer**, T. Broughton; Gy 1046 **Rolls Royce**, Bannisters; Gy 1046 **Rilette**, E. and R. Cox; Gy 1048 **Carbineer II**, Consols; Gy 1056 **Eider**,Trawlers WS and Gy; Gy 1060 **Okino,** Diamond Steam Fishing; Gy 1063 **Refundo**, R. Humphrey; Gy 1070 **Lanchester**, Bannisters; Gy 1073 **Sea Hawks**, E. Sheldon; Gy 1076 **Hugelia**, Baskcomb; Gy 1076 **Jon Grey**, John Lewis; Gy 1080 **Olympia**, Geat Grimsby and East Coast; Gy 1082 **Vambery**, Atlas Steam Fishing; Gy 1084 **Egret**, Baskcomb; Gy 1085 **Atlanti**, W.Lamberty; Gy 1088 **Pelham**, Earl Steam Fishing; Gy 1096 **Buckingham**, Queen Steam Fishing; Gy 1097 **Drummer**, Consols; Gy 1100 **Carbill**, J. Smethurst; Gy 1101 **Pegusus**, Lindsey Steam Fishing; Gy 1103 **Researcho**, Sleights; Gy 1104 **Oswaldian**, Loyal Steam Fishing; Gy 1107 **Dinorah**, Bowering Steam Fishing; Gy 1109 **Robert George**, A. Osbourne; Gy 1112 **Sylvia**, Forward Steam Fishing; Gy 1113 **Macleay**, Consols; Gy 1121 **Pearl**, T. C. and F. Moss; Gy 1138 **Tubal Cain**, Bunch; Gy 1141 **Quassia**, Baskcomb; Gy 1144 **Dinske**, Garratt and Jeffs; Gy 1146 **Rinto** and Sleights; Gy 1147 **Robina**, Baskcomb; Gy 1154 **Serapion**, Diamond Steam Fishing; Gy 1155 **Scooper**, Lindsey Steam Fishing; Gy 1157 **Ranere**, Bowering Steam Fishing; Gy 1160 **Rugby**, Grimsby Trawler Owners; Gy 1167 **Slasher**, Lindsey Steam Fishing; Gy 1168 **Ennerdale**, T. Brown;Gy 1170 **Dargle**, Garratt; Gy 1176 **Irwell**, Garratt and Jeffs; Gy 1177 **Lavinia**, Lindsey Steam Fishing; Gy 1179 **Orvicto**, Northern Steam Fishing; Gy 1189 **Croxton**, T and F Moss; Gy 1193 **Snowstorm**, Garratt and Jeffs; Gy 1194 **Goshawk II**, Baskcomb; Gy 1197 **Queen**, Queen Steam Fishing; Gy 1198 **Guillmont**, Baskcomb; Gy 1201 **Victor**, Dobson Steam Fishing; Gy 1202 **Lucerne**, C. Dobson; Gy 1208 **Rodrigo**, Sleights; Gy 1218 **Editor**, C. Dobson; Gy 1219 **Akranes**, Baskcomb and Northcote; Gy 1220 **Ophir III**, Crampins; Gy 1221 **Sea Lion**, TWS and Gy; Gy 1226 **Oliver Curphey**; Gy **1226 Runnell**, Baskcomb; Gy 1227 **Our Tena**, C. Dobson; Gy 1228 **Hawthorne**, Grant and Robinson; Gy 1229 **Collingwood**, Dobson; Gy 1230 **Heron**, Baskcomb; Gy 1232 **Rosco,**Sleights; Gy 1224 **Roarena**, Sleights; Gy 1235 **Elk**, Victorisan Steam Fishing; Gy 1236 **Reindeer**, Garratt; Gy 1240 H and B Trawlers; Gy 1241 **Sturton**, Victorian Steam Fishing; Gy 1242 **Precurser**, A. Priestly; Gy 1244 **Bonnie Bell**, G. Osbourne; Gy 1246 **Pride of the Humber**, A. Priestly; Gy 1247 **Elf King**, Grant and Baker; Gy 1248 **Forget-me-not**, W and C Harper; Gy 1251 **Sea King,** Grant and Baker; Gy 1254 Spider, Grant and Baker; Gy 1255 **North King** II, Grant and Baker; Gy 1260 **Equator**, Dobson; Gy 1267 **Righto**, Sleights; Gy 1275 **Nubia**, Grimsby and East Coast Steam Fishing; Gy 1276 **Maud Powell**, R.Bland; Gy 1277 **Natal II**, Diamond Steam Fishing; Gy 1278 **Carlton**, T. and F. Moss; Gy 1279 **Bonheur**, W. Johnson; Gy 1281 **Brisbane**, Dobsons; Gy 1285 **Edinboro Castle** Bannister and Barton; Gy 1287 **Enderby**, Dobson; Gy 1288 **Conway**, T. and F. Moss; Gy 1290 **Chandos**, Trawlers WS and Gy; Gy 1293 **Succession**, Lees; Gy 1296 **Heat Wave**, Garratt; Gy 1306 **Xylopia**, Baskcomb; Gy 1308 **Tasconia**, Dobsons';Gy 1309 **Syringa**, Dobsons: Gy 1310 **Rosa**, Dobsons: Gy 1314 **Annabelle**, Consols; Gy 1315 **Arlette**, Consols; Gy

1321 **William Hanbury**, *Taylors;* Gy 1323 **Joseph and Mary**, *J. Campbell;* Gy 1326 **Hennette**, Gy 1327 **Delila**, Gy 1329 *Sabina*, Gy 1330 **Suzette**, Gy 1331 *Evelina*, Gy 1332 **Yolando**, Gy 1333, *Soubrette*, Gy 1334 **Crevette**, Gy 1335 **Flavia**, Gy 1336 **Mirabelle**, Gy 1337 **Ninette**, *all Consols;* Gy 1341 **Savaria**, *Crofts;* Gy 1342 **Yesso**, *Diamond Steam Fishing;* Gy 1344 **Croton**, *Baskcomb;* Gy 1346 **City of London**, Gy 1347 **City of Glasgow**, Gy 1348 **City of Perth**, Gy 1350 **City of Edinburgh**, Gy 1351 **City of Hull**, *all Drifters Ltd;* Gy 1355 **Unity**, *H.Kirman.*

Memorial Panel: Central Hall, Grimsby.

In the Fisherman's Chapel situated in the Central Hall, Grimsby, there is a memorial board upon which are inscribed details of ships and men lost from the port during peacetime and wartime since 1914. The centre panel is carved in marble and depicts the figure of a woman who is comforting her child in what seems to have been a very familiar setting in Grimsby – the mourning of a husband and father. Details of the sculpture show the woman and her child dressed in the fashion of the day with a touching attention to detail; the woman's bootlace is undone, her face lined with mourning. The roll of honour on each side of the carving contains numbers and names of ships lost from Grimsby during the period 1914–1919. That list alone contains 71 trawlers and the 606 crewmen who sailed on their final fishing voyages from the port, never again to be seen.

Then there are the mine sweepers, many of them trawlers which had been requisitioned by the Admiralty. No vessel's names are mentioned but this list shows that another 429 men died in their country's service. After 1919, the intention was to carry on the tradition of adding names of men and ships, so additional boards were affixed on each side of the War memorial. The first losses are dated 15 May, 1920 and between then and September 1975, there were recorded 31 complete trawler crews who were lost at sea. Those and other losses total 815 men who lost their lives in the pursuit of fish for the tables of Britain. It is a very sobering thought that between 1914 and 1975, 102 trawlers and an undisclosed number of mine sweepers were lost while a total of 1,750 men perished while going about their business upon our great waters.

CAN YOU HELP?

GRAND OLD LADIES - VOLUME 2 will be published next year. If you have any photographs or stories of the fishermen or trawlers of Grimsby or the surrounding area, they may be of interest to us with a view to possible inclusion in our next publication.

If you think you may be able to help, please send your material to the address below. We regret that we are only able to return material if you enclose the appropriate sized SAE.

Thanking you

Research Dept
Archive Publications Ltd
10 Seymour Court, Manor Park, Runcorn, Cheshire WA7 1SY Telephone: 0928-567903

Listed below is the title backlist published by Archive Publications Ltd. They are available from most local book retailers, but if you encounter any problem locating a title, please do not hesitate to contact us at the above address.

Grimsby at War	Clive Hardy		£6.95
Nottingham at War	Nigel Arthur/Clive Hardy		£7.95
Scotland at War	Ian Nimmo		£7.95
Teesside at War	Malcolm Race		£7.95
Plymouth at War	Keith Scrivener		£6.95
Sheffield at War	Clive Hardy		£5.95
Memories of Swansea at War			£3.95
Tyneside at War	Clive Hardy/Paul Harris		£5.95
Aberdeen FC	Alistair Guthrie		£6.95
Burnley FC	Tony Durkin		£6.95
Notts County FC	David McVay		£6.95
Nottingham Forest FC	Duncan Hamilton		£6.95
The Wolves	Martin Swain		£7.95
Blackburn Rovers FC	Peter White		£6.95
Everton FC	Ric George		£7.95
Swansea City FC	John Burgum		£6.95
Grimsby Town FC	Geoff Ford		£8.95
Scunthorpe United FC	Bob Steels		£8.95
Wigan RLFC	Leslie Woodhead		£8.95
Widnes RLFC	Leslie Woodhead		£8.95
Nottingham CCC	Nick Lucy		£6.95
Who's Who in British Athletics	Peter Matthews		£8.95
The Golden 80s — A Decade of the Cheltenham Gold Cup	John Drinkwater		£9.95
Bygone Merseyside	Derek White		£4.95
Edinburgh: The Fab 50's	Paul Harris		£7.95
Leicester in the Fifties			£7.95
Nottingham Then	Ralph Gee		£6.95
Bygone Gloucester	Bill Brunt		£7.95
Disaster!	Paul Harris	£12.95 h/b	£7.95
Edinburgh Then	Hamish Coghill		£7.95
Rotherham Memory Lane	John Tunney		£4.95
Aberdeen Since 1900	Paul Harris		£6.95
Burnley Since 1900	Keith Fort		£6.95
Swansea Since 1900	Nigel Arthur		£6.95
Blackburn Since 1900	David Allin		£6.95
Edinburgh Since 1900	Paul Harris		£6.95
Sheffield Since 1900	Peter Harvey		£7.95
Glasgow Since 1900	Paul Harris		£7.95
Tyneside Since 1900	Clive Hardy		£6.95
Bumbles of Mumbles	Alexandra Firth		£4.95
Manchester Jewry	Bill Williams		£6.95
Israel at Forty	Paul Harris		£6.95
Manchester Fire Brigade	Robert Bonner		£7.95
THE POLICE! 150 Years of Policing in the Manchester Area	Duncan Broady/Carol Sawkil		£8.95
By Appointment	Paul Harris	£12.95 h/b	£6.95